The Alternative Empire

The Alternative Empire

Tom Wilson

Contents

Chapter 1

Empires Then and Now

Although we may not realise it, we all live surrounded by an empire, by which I mean power structures that contain us and direct us. The society in which Jesus and the first disciples lived was controlled by the Roman Empire. Today the empire is not quite so obvious, but no less powerful. Brian Walsh and Sylvia Keesmaat in their book *Colossians re:mixed*, quote a few examples that make this point quite clearly. In his 1994 annual report, the president of Campbell's Soup Company wrote, 'As I look forward to the future, I shiver with business excitement. That's because Campbell's Soup Company is engaged in a global consumer crusade.' The CEO and president of Wal-Mart, David Glass, explains that Wal-Mart's priorities are 'to dominate North America first, the South America, and then Asia and then Europe.'[1] Those plans sound to me like military strategy, the plans of empires to dominate the world.

---

[1] Brian J. Walsh and Sylvia C. Keesmaat. (2005). *Colossians re:mixed: Subverting the Empire*. Milton Keynes: Paternoster, p.166.

Think, for example, about who controls what is published in newspapers, who decides what gets airtime on the radio, which programmes (and adverts) dominate the television. Think about how a small number of large multinational companies actually own far more brands than you might realise. Brian Walsh and Sylvia Keesmaat suggest that we can probably tell as much about the real spirituality and real worldview of any individual or group of people in the developed work by looking at the cars they drive, the food they consume, the gadgets that fill their houses, the rubbish they throw away as we can by listening to the songs they sing, or the prayers they say.[2] Everyone chooses what they worship and we live in an empire just as much as Jesus did. The purpose of this short book is to help you begin to think about how Jesus and his first followers responded to the empire that surrounded them. This will, I hope, better equip you to respond to the empire that surrounds you each and every day. I do not want to encourage conspiracy theories or paranoia, just help you think a bit more about how to live with Jesus as your number one priority.

This opening chapter describes the society in which the first Christians lived. I outline the experience of Christians and how they began to build an alternative empire to the one that surrounded them. The chapter ends with some reflections on how we can do the same in contemporary society.

The Society The First Christians Lived In

It is generally agreed that the society the first Christians lived in was very rigidly organised, with a small social elite and a small group at the very bottom of the social scale, and the vast majority of the population in the middle. The precise figures for the elite do vary, but are generally considered

[2] Walsh and Keesmaat, *Colossians re:mixed*, p.199.

to be around, if not slightly less than, one percent of the total population.[3] This tiny portion of the population was made up of three groups: senators, equestrians and decurions, all of whom were hugely wealthy. Bible scholar Philip Esler states that a senator had to possess at least 250 000 denarii, an eques, 'somewhat less than half that amount,' and a decurion 25 000 denarii.[4] Since a denarius was a day's wages for a labourer, these were all considerable sums of money, although much of this wealth was held in the form of land. If we wanted a comparison with today, and said a labourer, working for 8 hours at just over the minimum wage, might earn £60 in a day, that would mean a senator had to be worth at least £15 million, a eques about £7 million and a decurion £1.5 million. The numbers do not quite do justice to the elite status of these people, but they give us some ideas. Having such fixed figures as the main criterion for entry into these groups ensured that their numbers were largely fixed, and their legal status further ensured their survival and consistent size.

At the opposite end of the social scale were those who had no position or status at all, the slaves. Slave labour was the backbone of the Roman economy. Since working to earn or maintain one's living was something well-off people hated the very the idea of, the wealthy relied exclusively on slaves to run their large estates, and so maintain their position within society.

Slaves were entirely the property of their masters, 'an animate piece of property, imprintable and disposable at the will of the master.'[5] Slaves were not human beings, but possessions, and furthermore, this position was likely to be maintained for their entire lives. Richard Horsley convincingly

---

[3] Wayne Meeks. (1988). *The Moral World of the First Christians.* Louisville: Westminster John Knox Press, p.33.

[4] Philip Esler (1989) *Community and Gospel in Luke Acts: The Social and Political Motivations of Lucan Theology.* Cambridge: Cambridge University Press, p.171.

[5] Richard Horsley, (2001). The Slave Systems of Classical Antiquity and Their Reluctant Recognition by Modern Scholars. *Semeia* 83/84: 19-66, p.30.

argues that cases of manumission (slaves buying freedom) were relatively rare; that when they did take place it was once the slaves were too old to make any significant personal economic gain; and that although it changed their legal status from slave to freedman/woman (that is, from non-person to one with limited rights), such slaves were normally left in a highly dependant patron-client relationship with their former owner.[6] So to be born a slave meant being a slave for all of your life.

The majority of the population was in between these two groups. This middle group were divided into four main different social groups as follows. First, the wealthier merchants and traders, who normally earned a reasonable living, together with artisans and those engaged in service industries, such as hauliers or bargemen. They all formed themselves into guilds or *collegia*. The second main group was that of unskilled workers, both free men and freed men, all of whom were dependant on finding employment, often on a day by day basis. Third, those unable to work had to live by begging. Finally, there were 'debt bondsmen,' who were technically not slaves. However, although creditors appear to have no legal right to force them to work off their debt, this does seem to have been the normal course of action, and so they were in effect slaves until they could clear their debts.[7]

Social mobility was relatively limited; there might be scope for movement between adjacent groups, but more dramatic social climbing was unheard of. It was, of course, possible to fall rapidly down the social scale, and end up a slave, although this was not that common. This suggests a largely static society, with relatively little opportunity for social climbing. But how did the first Christians fit in?

[6] Richard Horsely, 'The Slave Systems of Classical Antiquity', pp.48-52.

[7] Philip Esler. (1989). *Community and Gospel in Luke Acts: The Social and Political Motivations of Lucan Theology*. Cambridge: Cambridge University Press, pp.173-74.

The Position Of Christians Within Greco-Roman Society

Some people were very scathing about Christians. For example, Celcus, a second-century opponent of Christianity described the preachers of Christianity as 'wool-workers, cobblers, laundry workers, and the most illiterate and bucolic of yokels.'[8]

This is probably exaggeration to make his point of hatred, and so not all scholars agree with the description; the generally accepted position is that with the exception of the one percent urban elite, Christianity reached all sections of society, even if many Christians were amongst the lower ranks of society.[9] Looking specifically at the congregations founded by the Apostle Paul, scholar Wayne Meeks acknowledges that the evidence is fragmentary and unclear, but that nevertheless, the following groups were all represented: Christians in the *familia Caesaris*, 'whose members were so often among the few upwardly mobile people in the Roman Empire' (Philippians 4:22); other freedmen or descendants of freedmen who have advanced in wealth and position, especially in Corinth and Philippi (Romans 16:23; Philippians 4:15-17); wealthy artisans and traders, that is to say people who were high in income, but low in prestige; wealthy independent women and wealthy Jews.[10]

This suggests there were Christians of virtually all of the social classes in the first century. There were more amongst the lower classes, but then there were more people in these social classes. Christianity did not especially impact the very elite, the richest of the rich, but in every other social class

---

[8] Origen *Contra Celcus* 3.55, English translation by Frederick Crombie.

[9] For example E. A. Judge (1960). *The Social Pattern of Christian Groups in the First Century*. London: Tyndale Press, pp.49-61.

[10]Wayne Meeks. (1982). The Social Context of Pauline Theology. *Interpretation* 36, p.270.

Christians were found. Christians were everywhere and so the Roman Empire had a real influence on their daily lives.

The Empire And The Emperor

One aspect of the Roman Empire that should not be under-estimated is the Imperial Cult, the worship of the Emperor as a God. In his book, *The Imperial Cult and the Development of Church Order*, Allen Brent observes that a big problem for the Roman authorities was not only that Christians claimed an allegiance to another, spiritual kingdom, but that in doing so, they were violating the divine law.[11] He explains the issue like this:

> When Virgil writes the Aeneid (29-19 B.C.), Augustus duly emerges as bringer of the golden age and at least destined for divinity. Trojan Caesar shall descend from Julius "who shall limit his empire with the ocean, and his fame with the stars." (1,287). When Venus his mother welcomes him to heaven, then, "the harsh ages shall soften when wars have ceased (*aspera tum postis mitescent saecula bellis*)." (1,291). Thus in the famous lines Virgil can sing the prophecy of the Sibyl heard in the underworld:
>
> > Hic vir, hic est, tibi quem promitti saepius audis,
> > Augustus Caesar, divi genus, aurea condet
> > saecula qui rursus Latin regnata per ana
> > Saturno quondam .... (6, 791, 794)

[11]Allen Brent (1999). *The Imperial Cult and the Development of Church Order: Concepts and Images of Authority in Paganism and Early Christianity Before the Age of Cyprian*. Leiden: Brill, p.7.

'This is the man, this is he whom you
have often heard promised,
Augustus Caesar, son of God, who shall
found the golden age
once more over the fields were Saturn
reigned...'[12]

Not only is Augustus described as a son of god, but in the Roman Imperial cult, the Emperor was thought of as able to act as both priest and god of his own cult and to sacrifice as it were to himself.[13] Phrases such as 'son of god,' 'saviour,' or 'king,' which we all readily associate with Jesus, were in the everyday language of Romans but used in reference to the Emperor. By proclaiming a different Lord, Christianity really did bring in an alternative empire, which subverted the powers of Rome.

Moreover, Roman religion did not just include worship of the Emperor as a god; there were also the gods of hearth and home. Brent describes how the hearth of the house was sacred, festooned with flowers at each phase of the lunar month. A sacred fire burned in the hearth. Each day the *paterfamilias* (the head of the household) offered a portion of food, assigned to the sacrificial flames, for the spirits of the departed of the family, who were the semi- divine.[14] Worship was everywhere, and every day Christians had to choose how they responded to the empire that surrounded them and the empire of their Saviour and Lord Jesus Christ. There were gods everywhere, and every day you had to choose whom you worshipped.

[12]Brent, *The Imperial Cult*, p.58.
[13]Brent, *The Imperial Cult* p.66.
[14]Brent, *The Imperial Cult*, p.62.

Building An Alternative Empire

Christians chose to worship only one God, and so Christianity built an alternative empire to the Roman Empire. The New Testament scholar Gerd Theissen suggests that the two basic values of the first-century Christian ethic were love of neighbour and renunciation of status,[15] two values that were the foundations of this new Christian empire.

Love of neighbour

Love of neighbour is, of course, a Jewish teaching, found in Leviticus 19:18 (see also Deuteronomy 5:10; 10:18-19; 11:1). Within the early Church, love of neighbour became love of enemy (Matthew 5:43-48), was extended to become love of the stranger (Luke 10:25-37) and became love of the sinner (Luke 7:36-50). In John's Gospel and Paul's letters, there is a hint that love of neighbour did become exclusive to the community of faith (John 13:34; 15:12, 17; Galatians 6:10), although this may be more because of whom those texts were written for than anything else.

The notion of love of neighbour was not exclusive to the Judaeo-Christian tradition. There are references in Greek authors to the same ideals:

> When someone commended the maxim of Cleomenes, who, on being asked what a good king ought to do, said, "To do good to his friends and evil to his enemies," Ariston said, "How much better, my good sir, to do good to our friends and to make friends of our enemies."[16]

[15]Gerd Theissen. (2010). *A Theory of Primitive Christian Religion*. London: SCM Press, pp.63-80.
[16]Plutarch, *Moralia*, 218A (English Translation by F. C. Babbitt).

So we cannot claim that only Christians tried to love their neighbours, nor can we say only Christians cared for those in need. But if we look into the situation in a little more detail, then some clear differences do emerge. The primary difference may be found in the fact that secular (that is non-Christian) giving was focused on elevating the status of the giver, whilst Christians were discouraged from such practices.

An example of secular giving, concerned primarily for personal gain, is the following inscription, from an Egyptian official:

> I did what men love and the gods praise, a true dignitary who had no fault. I gave bread to the hungry, clothes to the naked; I was one who drove away suffering and warded off need, who buried the honourable and cared for the old, who drove away the distress of those with nothing, a shade for the orphan, a helper for the widows, who bestowed office on one who was still in swaddling clothes...[17]

So this Egyptian offical has done a lot of good stuff, but the purpose of the inscription is to tell you that he is the one who did it. It appears the main aim of his acts of generosity was to elevate his own status, to make sure everyone knew of his power and wealth. Christians, by contrast, were encouraged to give to those from whom they might expect no reward, although such giving tended to focus on the wider Christian community (for example 1 Corinthians 16:1-4; 2 Corinthians 8-9; 1 John 3:17-18). This was the Christian ideal, even if in reality giving may not always have been so selfless (as Acts 5:1-11 indicates). Love of neighbour was, for the Christian, not for personal gain, but for the glory of God and in response to the love God had shown (1 John 3:16-18).

[17]Quoted in Theissen, *A Theory of Primitive Christianity*, pp.91-92.

Renouncing status

The second value of the early Church, of renouncing status, can be understood in three different ways. First, at the most basic level of humility, as commended in James 1:9-11. Thus the one who has lowly status inwardly accepts it and the one who has high status does not exploit it. Second, those who have higher status renounce the use of that higher status to impose their will, or preferably third, renunciation of the status itself, humbling oneself to exalt others (Luke 13:22-30; 1 Corinthians 9:19-23).

Christians were urged to imitate Jesus, as Paul makes clear in his letter to the Philippians (2:5-11), and lower their own social status. As with the command to love neighbour and give selflessly, not all Christians were prepared to renounce their status. Paul's command in 1 Corinthians 7:17-24 is just one example of his challenges to the desire for social mobility and status, in which he argues that such things are not to be sought after. The reason it was so difficult was that everyone else was engaged in being upwardly mobile, and there was a strong temptation to try and keep up. To give but one example, in his recollection of his career, the writer Lucian explains why he chose to pursue education over training as a sculptor, since the latter would be entirely insignificant in public.[18]

Everyone was interested in making a name for themselves, in building a reputation. In choosing to ignore their own gain, Christians really were being counter-cultural, and so building an entirely different empire from the one which surrounded them.

[18]Lucian, *The Dream or Lucian's Career*. (Loeb Classical Library, Lucian Volume III, English translation by A. M. Harmon, pp.214-33)

Empires Today

If we are truly honest, is modern British society really all that different from first-century Roman society as I have described it above?

The executive summary of a recent report *Below the Breadline* reads as follows:[19]

> The UK is the seventh richest country in the world. It is also a deeply unequal country. In May 2014, the Office for National Statistics (ONS) reported that the richest one percent of Britons own the same amount of wealth as 54 percent of the population. The same month, the Sunday Times reported that the 1,000 richest people in the country had doubled their wealth in five years.
>
> Yet at the same time, millions of families across the UK are living below the breadline. Oxfam and Church Action on Poverty have calculated that 20,247,042 meals were given to people in food poverty in 2013/14 by the three main food aid providers. This is a 54 percent increase on 2012/13.
>
> Protecting its citizens from going hungry is one of the most fundamental duties of government. Most of us have grown up with the assumption that when we fall on hard times, the social security safety net will kick in and prevent us from falling into destitution and hunger. The principle

[19]*Below the Breadline: The relentless rise of Food Poverty in Britain* (June 2014), published jointly by Oxfam, Church Action on Poverty and the Trussel Trust. The executive summary is on page 4, where references to the sources cited can be found.

of this crucial safety net now appears to be under threat.

Food banks are a service of last resort for people living in poverty. As the authors of a report commissioned by the Department for Environment, Food and Rural Affairs (DEFRA) on food poverty stated: 'There is no evidence to support the claim that increased food aid provision is driving demand. All available evidence, both in the UK and internationally, points in the opposite direction. Put simply, there is more need and informal food aid providers are trying to help.'

People on low incomes have traded down and down again to the cheapest food products; after which they simply have to buy less food. We have spoken to people living on one meal a day, drinking hot water and lemon to tame hunger pangs, trying to think how they can survive on a household budget of £6 a week. More than half a million children in the UK are now living in families who are unable to provide a minimally acceptable diet.

Despite their best efforts, many people cannot earn enough to live on. UK food prices have increased by 43.5 per cent in the eight years to July 2013 and food expenditure as a proportion of total household expenditure has continued to rise. The UK has one of the highest levels of housing costs in Europe, while between 2010 and 2013 energy prices for households rose by 37 per cent. At the same time, low and stagnant wages, insecure and zero-hours contracts mean that for many low-income households, the money they are bringing home is less every month than their essential outgoings.

Evidence shows that changes to the social security system are a driver of food poverty. Cuts to social security since April 2013 have had a severe impact on poor and vulnerable families across the UK. These cuts have been coupled with an increasingly strict and often misapplied sanctions regime—58 percent of sanctions decisions are successfully challenged, suggesting that many people needlessly suffer a loss of income through no fault of their own. The abolition of the Social Fund has prevented thousands of households from being able to access crisis loans. The Trussell Trust, the largest food bank network in the UK, estimates that 49 percent of people referred to food banks are there due to problems with social security payments or because they have been refused a crisis loan.

In the last year, the All Party Parliamentary Group (APPG) on Hunger and Food Poverty has been set up with broad cross-party political support, and is conducting an Inquiry into the issue. The Work and Pensions Select Committee has considered the link between social security reforms and the increased use of food aid. These developments are welcome.

However, far more needs to be done and with a greater sense of urgency. The government is failing more broadly to properly investigate or address the causes of the significant increase in food bank use. While we welcome the APPG Inquiry into the issue, this should not be used as an excuse for inaction at a wider level. All political parties must clearly commit to urgent action if we are to begin to tackle the growing problem of food poverty in the UK.

This is simply one report into one aspect of a big, big problem. We live in an empire whose social structure increasingly reminds me of the Roman Empire: a rich elite, a forgotten underbelly and everyone in the middle struggling to survive. As Christians today, how will we respond? What empire do we seek to serve? The gods of consumerism, of personal gain, of getting the best job, the nicest car? The gods of political correctness, of refusing to upset anyone by suggesting that Jesus Christ is the only way to salvation? The temptations are there, even if the gods are more subtle than they were in Roman times.

In each the next six chapters, I will do three things. First, I will briefly outline how different aspects of Biblical teaching present an alternative empire to the one of the day. The chapters examine the four Gospels (Matthew, Mark, Luke and John), the teaching of the Apostle Paul, and the book of Revelation. Then having given a short outline, I will introduce a particular passage in more detail. Finally, I will suggest how we can live in an alternative empire today, living out that same subversion in our own context.

Chapter 2

Mark And Empire

'Down with the Roman Empire! Up with Jesus!' That is one statement you will not find anywhere in Mark's Gospel. It is not written as a manifesto of a political or guerilla movement challenging the power of the Roman Empire. But Mark's Gospel does, in its own way, set out an alternative empire, one where Jesus reigns, where the might of Rome is of little consequence, and where different values are the most important.

Although no one can be completely sure, many people (including myself) think that Mark was probably the first of the four Gospels to be written. There are many reasons for this, and the main one is the length of the Gospels. Mark is the shortest, but at the same time the individual stories he tells are often longer and with more details. It seems likely that he wrote first, and then Matthew and Luke followed roughly the same order as Mark, but omitted some of the details because they were already recorded. John follows an entirely different structure, and personally I think he wrote it in his old age, as a complement to the other three Gospels.

15

According to Church tradition, Mark records the Apostle Peter's accounts of his time with Jesus, and Mark is noticeably quite harsh in how he describes the first disciples: Matthew and Luke soften the blows somewhat. This is another reason why many people think Mark was written first, as it makes more sense for the things Jesus says to be made less, rather than more, harsh.

This short book is not the place to go into the detail of the order in which the Gospels were written, and it does not matter too much. I included the paragraph above to explain why I have begun with Mark, not Matthew. What is important is the movement that we will be doing in each chapter: we will move between the two horizons of the text: the horizon of the original context, and the horizon of the contemporary context. Mark made many assumptions about what his first listeners knew, thought and understood. Everyone does this when they tell stories. To give an example, to which I will return, in 8:27, Mark assumes that when he mentions Caesarea Philippi his readers know that he is referring to a city that used to be called Paneas of Panion, and had recently been enlarged by the local ruler Herod Philip and renamed Caesarea in honour of Augustus, who had given control of the city to Herod, Philip's father.[1] This makes the reference to Jesus as Lord in this city a much more subversive and challenging statement than it may at first appear.

The problem for us is that we don't think in quite the same way as Mark, and as we read his Gospel, we need to move backwards and forwards, from his context to our context, to try and establish the similarities and differences that will help us understand the empire he imagines, the empire he wants us to try and realise in our world today.

The structure of this, and the next five chapters, will be the same. First I will give a short overview of the book as

[1] R. T. France. (2002). *The New International Greet Testament Commentary: The Gospel of Mark.* Carlisle: Paternoster, p.327.

a whole, highlighting how it sets out the alternative empire where Jesus is Lord. Second, I will look at a particular passage in more depth, before third telling a contemporary fictional story to illustrate some of the principles I've discussed in the chapter so far.

Jesus Is Lord

There is no doubt at all who Mark thinks Jesus is. The opening sentence of the Gospel makes that quite plain. He starts with 'The beginning of the good news about Jesus Christ.' Some manuscripts add 'the Son of God,' in case you had not worked that out as well. There is absolutely no doubt in Mark's mind that he is telling you about a new King. Remember he is writing in a time when Emperors claimed that title for themselves. So although you may not have recognised it as such, this opening sentence is, in fact, a statement of an alternative empire, something that is echoed a few verses latter, when Jesus says, 'The time is fulfilled, the kingdom of God has drawn near; repent and believe the good news.' Jesus himself tells us that he has brought in this new empire, and he wants us to turn, to change, and to commit ourselves to following him wholeheartedly.

Bible scholar Ched Myers argues very strongly that Mark's Gospel is a political book, written 'to help imperial subjects learn the hard truth about their world and themselves. ... His is a story by, about, and for those committed to God's work of justice, compassion, and liberation to the world.'[2] It is the story of a new world order, not one imposed by invasion, by top-down force, but one that grows inexorably, person by person, as lives are changed, person

---

[2] Ched Myers. (2008). *Binding the Strong Man: A Political Reading of Mark's Story of Jesus.* Maryknoll: Orbis Books, p.11.

by person and group by group, as unjust structures are challenged and reformed, and kingdom values begin to reign.

In common with most scholars, Myers divides Mark's Gospel into two main parts.[3] The crucial 'hinge' on which the Gospel turns is 8:22-38, where Jesus heals a blind man, Peter declares Jesus is the Messiah, and then Jesus teaches exactly what that means. This is the passage I will discuss in more detail below, but first I will outline the structure that Myers proposes for the whole of Mark.

Myers sub-divides the first half of Mark's Gospel into five: first a prologue and call to discipleship (1:1-20). Second comes Jesus' assault of the Jewish social order in Capernaum (1:21-3:35). In this section the main focus is on how Jesus' teachings, healings and association with the socially excluded bring him into conflict with the authorities. The stage is set for a conflict of power. In part three, Jesus gives a sermon on revolutionary patience (4:1-36). Parables of listening and watching remind us of the public nature of God's kingdom, but also of the different structure and order it follows. The sower's radical generosity in sowing seed where it may not be fruitful challenges our desire to act only for personal gain and self-interest. Part four is part of Jesus' construction of a new social order (4:36-8:9). Here Jesus heals, feeds and travels, demonstrating inclusion and compassion, controlling nature and welcoming all regardless of social status, race or gender. Myers suggests part five is partially included in part four, as he regards the execution of John the Baptist (6:1-32) and the 'first epilogue' (7:1-23; 8:10-21) as being one unit together.

Myers sub-divides the second half of Mark's Gospel into six parts. The first is the second prologue and call to discipleship (8:22-9:30) which I will discuss in greater detail below.

---

[3] All of what follows comes from Myers *Binding the Strong Man*. Some is just listing the contents pages and some is based on discussion within. I have not referenced every idea in order to make it easier to read. The structure and explanation are all Myers'.

Second, there is another section of teaching on the new social order (9:30-10:52). This section puts flesh on the bones of Jesus' 'way of the cross.' Jesus explains what it means to resist without violence, to serve without a desire for personal gain, to put the least first, and the powerful last. Much of what society values is reduced in significance, and much of what we belittle is held up as valuable. In part three, Jesus comes to Jerusalem, and as he challenged the authorities in Capernaum, so now he challenges those in Jerusalem (11:1-13:3). There are symbolic actions (the entry into the city, the Temple cleansing, the cursing of the fig tree) and direct confrontations with scribes and Pharisees. In part four Jesus gives another sermon on revolutionary patience (13:4-37). Jesus warns his disciples against any rash desires to seize power and in a complex chapter interweaves predictions related to the more immediate future with information about his second coming to judge the world. In part five Jesus is arrested and tried by the powers (14:1-15:20). The authorities conspire against him and his disciples betray him and flee from him. Jesus is alone against the authorities, and at this point they appear to have triumphed. But part six reminds us that the story is not finished with Jesus' arrest. He is executed and there is a 'second epilogue' (15:21-16:8). Myers argues that the abrupt ending is deliberate: it forces the reader to return to the beginning of the story, to think again about who this Jesus is. And it offers us a choice: will we flee in fear, or will we follow in faith? We may not understand all of what Jesus' resurrection signifies, but do we trust enough to devote our lives to him?

Spit In Your Eye

In his strikingly titled academic article 'Spit in Your Eye,' Bible scholar Eric Eve draws comparisons between the Roman Emperor Vespasian's purported healing miracle and one of the two times in Mark's Gospel (7:31-37; 8:22-26) when Jesus heals blind men by spitting.[4] Vespasian became Emperor in 69AD, in the midst of an empire in revolutionary turmoil. He needed to consolidate his position of power, and one of his strategies was to spread a story of how he healed a blind man by spitting. When Vespasian was in the city of Alexandria, the story went, a blind man came to him, saying that the god Sarapis had given him a vision that Vespasian would heal him by moistening his cheeks and eyes with spittle. Vespasian was initially reluctant, but was eventually persuaded. The healing was public, which is a contrast with the story in Mark's Gospel of the man Jesus healed at Bethsaida. Eve suggests it is quite possible that Mark wanted his first audience to notice the contrast with the story of Vespasian healing a man, one which they would doubtless have been familiar with.

This is the section of Mark's Gospel that I will examine in some detail, to bring out the idea of an alternative empire into clearer focus. The passage is as follows:

> They came to Bethsaida. Some people brought a blind man to Jesus and begged him to touch him. Jesus took the blind man by the hand and led him outside the village. He spat on his eyes, put his hands on them and asked him, "Can you see anything?"
>
> Looking up he said, "I can see people—they look like trees walking around."
>
> Once more Jesus put his hands on the man's eyes: his sight was restored, and he could see everything clearly. Then Jesus sent him home, saying, "Don't go into the village."
>
> Jesus and his disciples went on from there, to the villages of Caesarea Philippi. On the way, he asked his

[4] Eric Eve. (2008). Spit in Your Eye: The Blind Man of Bethsaida and the Blind Man of Alexandria. *New Testament Studies*. 54: 1-17.

> disciples, "Who do people say that I am?" They replied, "Some say John the Baptist, others Elijah, others one of the prophets." He asked them, "But who do you say that I am? Peter answered him, "You are the Christ."
>
> Jesus warned them not to tell anyone about him.

Mark 8:22-30

It seems likely that Mark is making a link between the healing miracle and the disciples' gradual realisation of whom Jesus is. The miracle comes in two stages: first people look like walking trees (that is, the man can only see indistinct, blurry shapes), and second the man's sight is fully restored. In the same way, first the disciples make faltering guesses at whom Jesus is before second Peter hits the nail on the head with his statement that Jesus is the Christ.

The suggestions regarding Jesus' identity reflect religious speculation of the day. The confusion over Jesus and John the Baptist has already occurred, and it can't be true because they have ministered together (see Mark 6:14-29). The link with Elijah comes from Old Testament prophecy. Elijah was a famous Old Testament prophet who spoke out to protect the people of God in a time of persecution under an ungodly king (see 1 Kings 17 to 2 Kings 2). He never died, but was taken up to heaven in a chariot of fire (2 Kings 2). Right at the end of the book of the prophet Malachi there is a promise that God would send Elijah back to prepare the world for God's coming judgement (Malachi 4:5-6). Elijah would call people to turn and repent, and usher in God's triumphant rule over the nations.

So the idea that Jesus was Elijah, or one of the prophets, or even John the Baptist, is very like the man seeing people like trees walking around. It is a partial perception; a half-seeing that does not quite get the point. Jesus is not the one who comes to prepare the world before the arrival of

God's kingdom; he is the God-man who has come to bring in the fullness of God's kingdom. It was John the Baptist who performed the Elijah role, and that stage in the process has already been completed. Thus Peter gets it right when he says that Jesus is the Christ or the Messiah, literally the 'anointed one,' anointed as a sign that he is set apart to be God's special agent and ambassador, as God's chosen king.

There are three reasons why this passage is also a challenge to the empire of the day. The first is the reason outlined above, that Vespasian, probably the Emperor at the time when Mark was writing, was using a very similar healing miracle as one of the ways of legitimising his own claim to power. The second is the location. They were heading towards Caesarea Philippi. As scholar Ben Witherington notes, Caesarea Philippi was a major city built in the far north of Galilee by Herod Philip to honour the Roman Emperor Augustus. Moreover, in ancient times it had been called Paneas in honour of the god Pan, and previously it had been a site where the god Baal was worshipped.[5] So in a city dedicated to false gods, including to the emperor as a god, Jesus' true identity was revealed. Third, the title, anointed one, Messiah or Christ, was understood in popular thought as the mark of a revolutionary leader who would come and overthrow the Roman Empire. Jesus recognises that he has come to do that, but not in the way Peter, or others expect. He has not come to lead a violent war, and so he will not let Peter—or anyone else—call him Messiah until they understand exactly what that means.

> Then he began to teach them that the Son of Man must suffer many things and be rejected by the elders, the chief priests and the teachers of the law, and that he must be killed and after three days, rise again. He spoke plainly to them about this. Peter took him to one side

[5] Ben Witherington III. (2001). *The Gospel of Mark: A Socio-Rhetorical Commentary.* Grand Rapids: Eerdmans, p.240.

> and began to rebuke him. But Jesus turned, and looking
> at his disciples, he rebuked Peter, "Get behind me Satan.
> You're not thinking of the things of God, but of people."
>
> Then he called the crowd to him along with his disciples,
> and said to them, "If any want to follow after me, let
> them deny themselves, take up their cross and follow
> me. For those who want to save their lives will loose
> them, but those who loose their lives for my sake and
> the sake of the gospel will save them. What's the use in
> gaining the whole world, if in the process you loose your
> very soul? Indeed, what would anyone give in return for
> their soul? If anyone is ashamed of me in this adulterous
> and sinful generation, then the Son of Man will also be
> ashamed of them when he comes in his Father's glory
> with the holy angels."

Mark 8:31-38

Jesus makes it clear that being God's chosen messenger does not mean you have a trouble free life. In fact it means almost exactly the opposite. The Son of Man is another of Jesus' phrases that hints about to his mission. It was a Hebrew and Aramaic idiom meaning 'human being' or 'person.' When Jesus uses it he is picking up on imagery in Daniel 7, where 'one like a son of man' (that is, a human being) is given power and authority to judge the world. And Jesus is now explaining that that power and authority to judge will be demonstrated by Jesus' suffering, rejection and death. This may well be because a true test of character is found in how we treat the vulnerable, those who can do nothing at all for us. Jesus comes amongst us as one who serves, and how we treat him is how we ourselves will be judged.

Unsurprisingly, this is all very confusing for Peter. He has just been told that he has correctly worked out that Jesus is God's chosen king, and so he's expecting Jesus to act like a king: to dominate, to crush his enemies, to establish his rule and authority with an iron fist. So all this talk about King Jesus suffering and dying is very worrying, and not something Peter wants to hear at all. Thus he tries to put a stop to it, but ends up being soundly told off. Being likened to Satan is about as blunt a rebuke as anyone could come up with!

But Jesus has to be blunt, because Peter is thinking in human terms, not in God's terms. Divine thinking is often counter-intuitive; as Jesus goes on to make clear. If we want to follow Jesus, we need to die, it is as simple as that. Now this is not a command to suicide or to deliberately seek martyrdom: but it is perhaps almost as painful. It is a demand that we die to our own ambitions, hopes, dreams, plans for the future, that we surrender all of them into Jesus' hands and leave him in total control. If we try to save ourselves, to take control of our own destiny, then we will ultimately perish, because that means we will die eternally separated from God, and face his judgement. But if we surrender everything to God, then he will take control of the situation, and we will not need to fear either the present or the future, but simply to trust in him, and he will show his faithfulness because Jesus will speak up for us at the final judgement, and we will be free.

This is Jesus' radical manifesto for his alternative empire, one where God is king, and where we serve him, and each other, without thought for our own personal gain or benefit. The first part of this section is entirely about Jesus, and his death for us. What follows is the application to our lives as individuals and as a group. It reminds us that Christianity is much more about what we do, how we live, how we treat other people and our planet, than it is about what we say we believe. We should live as citizens of a society where we are not interested in our own advancement, but only in the progress of God's kingdom.

Now some people will read this as an instruction to do themselves down, but it does not say this at all. While we are called to serve, we are not called to self-hatred or self-harm. Others will think that as long as what they are doing is 'for Jesus,' it does not matter who gets hurt or what the long term consequences are. That is equally false. How we treat others is supremely important. The long term fruit of our actions is the surest way to judge them. And love for Jesus does mean death to our own pride or ambitions, but it is not a reason to hate ourselves or be unnecessarily harsh in how we judge ourselves or others.

Questions

1. What links does Mark make between the story of the blind man being healed and the disciples' slow realisation of whom Jesus is?

2. In what ways does Mark set out an alternative empire in this passage?

3. How does that apply to us today?

4. How do you understand the idea of dying to yourself and following Jesus? What do you find easy and what do you find hard about doing this?

Cycling, Chocolate And Jesus

'What do you mean Jesus cares about cycling?' Richard asked, reaching forward to pick up his sandwich. He bit hard, and a small trail of tuna mayonnaise burst for freedom from the other end of roll, colonising his hand. Richard licked it off and looked at me expectantly.

'Well, think about it, Rich,' I replied. 'Jesus tells us to love our neighbours, right, and that includes everyone, even the granny you nearly mow down when you jump onto the pavement and swerve across the pelican crossing to avoid stopping at the red light.'

'I guess so,' he replied. 'But you know what a pain it is to stop with clip in shoes. Its such a hassle.'

'Hassle, sure,' I agreed, stabbing at my pasta. 'Dangerous and anti-social and not exactly Christian as well. What's more,' I added, going in for the kill while Richard munched on another mouthful of tuna and bread, 'it's not just about red lights. There's the question of how much time you spend out cycling when you could be hanging out with your kids, or indeed, how much you spend on a bike when there are thousands, no millions, who have no food, clothing or decent toilets. It all joins up.'

'Man, this being a Christian isn't easy is it?' Rich shook his head, and took a sip of his coffee. 'I mean, I get the whole love God with everything—what was it? Prayer, passion, intelligence, energy; that's what the speaker said at that service the other week. But every detail of my life? I have to open it all up to Jesus and let him be involved with every single thing? Now that's going to take some work.'

'Sure it is.' I leant forward slightly, a forkful of pasta in my hand, trying to avoid dropping tomato sauce on my shirt. 'Sure it is. Learning to live as a Christian is a life-long process. It's not a quick fix, one shot and you're perfect. You see bit by bit, gradually the light dawns on another part of your life, and you have to let Jesus take control of that as well. Let me tell you about me and chocolate to explain.'

'Go on,' Rich waved a welcoming hand, indicating his willingness to listen. He knew I loved chocolate. Sadly he also knew where I kept my 'secret' stash. 'Secret' in the sense that most of the office knew where it was, and often helped themselves when there was an emergency, like one of them felt a bit hungry, bored or wanted to annoy me.

'Well, you know I quite like chocolate...'

'"Quite like" in the sense of "can't get through a day without"?'

'Yeah, okay. I eat chocolate every day—which is why I cycle to work, as you know. But several years ago, when the fair trade campaign started to get serious, God spoke to me about chocolate.'

'What do you mean?' Rich was incredulous. 'Why would he care?'

'Oh, it wasn't a voice in the sky, no thunder or lightning, nothing dramatic. Just a growing sense of unease as I bought whatever chocolate I wanted. I started to think about how it was made, you know, about the people who grew the cocoa, who grew the sugar cane, all getting a fair wage. So I made a resolution; I would only buy fair trade chocolate. It was an expensive choice—especially in the early days when hardly any chocolate was fair trade. I cannot tell you how happy I was when Malteasers became fair trade. Changed my life; well, a bit, anyway.'

'So let me get this right,' Rich asked as he swallowed his last mouthful of his tuna roll, 'You think God told you that you had to only buy fair trade chocolate in order to be a proper Christian, and you're damned if you don't?'

'No, not that serious,' I held up both hands to slow Rich down, 'No, I'm not part of the fair trade police, those people who tut at the sight of non-fair trade tea. No, what I mean is, as I was thinking about my life, my habits, what I enjoy and what I'm doing with my money, I got a sense that Jesus was saying to me that I should try and only buy chocolate made fairly, where everyone is treated with dignity. I mean, we all moan when work takes the mick, don't we—you know, when you're expected to stay late with no time in lieu, no extra pay. So if it wasn't fair for that to happen to me, why

27

would it be fair for that to happen to the guy who grew the cocoa and sugar for my chocolate habit? Like you say, I eat enough of it, so I shouldn't exploit people.'

'Oh, I get it, so it's more a personal choice than a command chiseled on tablets of stone.' Rich nodded to himself, and took a swig of his coffee before peeling his second banana of the day. 'But what if someone buys you other chocolate?'

'Well, then I eat it, of course,' I grinned. 'If people ask, I ask them to buy fair trade, and my family all know that's what I want. But I don't make a huge fuss. It's just that when I can make a choice for a fairer world, where I can make a choice to love a neighbour I don't know, then I want to make that choice. But cycling is all for me.'

Rich and I both loved to cycle. It was one of the things that started us chatting to each other in the office, one of the ways I'd got to know him and started him thinking about following Jesus for himself. He was much more committed, with a better bike and all the gear, but I had enough decent stuff to be able to hold my own.

'So is that why you've still got the same bike after all those years,' Rich wanted to know, 'Because you think Jesus doesn't want you to buy a new one?'

'Well, I can't afford a new one—we give too much money away, and this one works just fine, that's true.' I agreed. 'And I cycle to stay fit—I think Jesus wants us to look after our own health, our own bodies, just as much as to love and care for others.'

'Well, that's good, as I love cycling,' Rich smiled. 'There's just so much to being a Christian. Every time we chat I discover something else to think about.'

'You remember the story of that blind man don't you—the one with the spit and "people like trees"?' I grinned, as

I can well remember Rich's disgust at the idea of spitting on someone's face to heal them.

He grinned back, remembering the same animated discussion many months ago. 'Yeah, bit by bit, our eyes are opened. I'd love to talk more, but I've gotta get back to it— I want to leave dead on five, so I can cycle the long way home.'

In this story I've tried to show two examples, one ongoing, and one in the past, of how individuals have their eyes opened to the need to surrender the whole of life to Jesus. Both are challenges to the culture—the empire—of the day.

In our present society, there is a tendency for people to consume what they want with no thought of those who produce it for us, and to travel where, how and when they want, again with little thought of the impact on others. Jesus calls us to be concerned for others, to give more than we take, to inconvenience ourselves for the good of others, and to love sacrificially.

What did the story make you think about? Are there areas of your life where you can only half-see, where Jesus is opening your eyes more fully to how he wants you to live?

Chapter 3

Matthew And Empire

Matthew is no more a fan of the Roman Empire than Mark. His longer account of Jesus' life is just as radical a subversion of the powers of the Empire. In particular, Matthew's record of Jesus' teaching sets out a clear alternative for how to live. It does not advocate violence, but neither does it recommend passive submission. Instead, the vision is of subversion, of working against the system from within, of exposing its flaws so that everyone can come to recognise a better way of living.

Matthew's Message Against The Empire

Scholar Warren Carter has written extensively arguing that Matthew's Gospel is written to help its first audience learn how to live as Christians in the face of the Roman Empire. He argues that these people lived in a world where negotiating Roman imperial power was a daily task. He suggests that perhaps Matthew's first audience lived in Antioch in Syria, which is at least a reasonable guess for where Matthew's Gospel was written. If true, then it was impossible to exist in that city without encountering numerous expressions of Roman imperial power: coins, buildings, troops, administrative officials, taxes, festivals.[1] According to Carter, the question Matthew's Gospel seeks to answer is: how should followers of Jesus, crucified by a Roman governor, negotiate the realities of living in the Roman Empire on a daily basis? Throughout Matthew, Jesus reveals and challenges the inadequacy of Roman rule. He presents an alternative vision, as he encourages alms-giving, acts mercifully, feeds the hungry, heals the sick and casts out demons. Jesus talks regularly about his empire, which Matthew calls 'the Kingdom of Heaven,' and challenges his followers to live in accordance with this empire's rules.

Carter argues that the whole of Matthew's Gospel is a guide to negotiating life in the Roman Empire.[2] He suggests it has six parts, and the central dynamic running through them all is the conflict between Jesus and the Rome-allied, Jerusalem based, leaders of the Jewish faith. He outlines the six parts as follows.

In part one (Matthew 1:1-4:16), God initiates the story in the conception and commissioning of Jesus to manifest God's saving presence. Jesus is threatened by Herod, witnessed to by John, sanctioned by God in baptism, tempted by the Devil, and validated by Scripture. Matthew's Gospel begins with a genealogy, establishing Jesus as a descendant of Abraham, chosen by God to be a blessing to all nations. The inclusion of five women in the list as well as flawed Jewish kings, such as Solomon, indicates that God's empire works to different standards than human empires. Throughout this opening section, Jesus encounters resistance, both from Herod and the

---

[1] Warren Carter. (2001). *Matthew and Empire: Initial Explorations.* London: T & T Clark, p.87

[2] Warren Carter. (2007). Matthew's Gospel: An Anti-Imperial/Imperial Reading. *Currents in Theology and Mission* 34(6) 423-433. What follows in this section is based on this article.

Devil's temptations. At the same time he receives approval: from John the Baptist's testimony, and most importantly, the affirmation of his ministry by his Father at his baptism.

In part two (Matthew 4:17-11:1), Jesus manifests God's saving presence, the empire or kingdom of God, by calling together a community of followers, preaching, healing, and exorcizing. Jesus calls his first followers, and then in the Sermon on the Mount (chapters 5 to 7) explains to them how their alternative empire will live by a different ethic. But this empire is not just about words; Jesus also acts to repair the damage done by Rome, healing the sick and driving out demons (chapters 8 and 9). The alternative empire is an empowering empire: Jesus sends out his followers to represent him and spread his message, warning them of the dangers and challenges they will face (chapter 10).

In part three (Matthew 11:2-16:20), Jesus' actions and words continue to reveal his identity as God's agent and the life giving purposes of God's empire. He draws positive and negative responses. Powerful elites conflict with him over his societal vision and practices. There are warnings of judgement for unrepentance, challenges to Jesus' ministry and authority, as his opponents compare him to the Beelzebul, the prince of demons. In a series of parables, Jesus explains the nature of the kingdom of heaven further (Matthew 13). He feeds and cares for both Jews and Gentiles, emphasising the inclusive nature of his kingdom. There is a clear priority to the alternative empire, in that Jesus came first and foremost to the Jews, but at the same time, everyone who trusts in God and wants to live with Jesus as king is welcomed into the kingdom of heaven.

In part four (Matthew 16:21-20:34), Jesus teaches his followers that conflict with the elite will result in his crucifixion in Jerusalem and God's raising of him from the dead. This event has numerous implications for their lives as followers. At the heart of the alternative empire is a belief in death and resurrection, and this begins with, and is centred on, Jesus himself. The message of his own immanent death is repeated three times in this section (16:21; 17:22-23; 20:17-19). Jesus reveals his own glory in the transfiguration (17:1-13), and warns of the upside-down values of his kingdom. In the alternative empire, all must become like children, there must be forgiveness and grace for every failure, and everyone will be rewarded for service, regardless of how long they have served the alternative empire.

In part five (Matthew 21:1-27:66), Jesus enters Jerusalem, challenges the center of the elite's power in the temple, gets into conflict with them over societal leadership, and condemns their world as temporary and facing imminent destruction under God's judgment. The alliance of Jerusalem leaders and the Roman governor crucifies him. The two empires clash. Entry processions by an emperor were always carefully choreographed displays of power; Jesus' entry into Jerusalem does so in a radically subversive way, proclaiming a kingdom of peace and grace. Jesus' actions in the temple reinforce the alternative empire's values of worship of God having priority over monetary gain. Jesus tells parables, condemning the rulers (21:28-22:14; 23:1-37), foretelling their demise (21:41; 22:7) and besting them in debate (22:15-46). In chapters 24 and 25, Jesus warns of the end of the age, when the Roman (and any other human) empire will fall, and all will be judged according to the standards of God's alternative empire. The inevitable clash of empires follows; the Roman and Jewish authorities plot together against Jesus and in a mockery of a show trial, he is condemned to death. It seems that human empires have triumphed as Jesus dies. But even in his moment of death, the power of the alternative empire is seen, as the temple curtain breaks, the holy people rise and the centurion, who represents the power of Rome, declares Jesus to be the Son of God (27:50-54).

In part six (Matthew 28:1-20), God's saving purposes overcome the worst that the elite can do and expose the limits of imperial power as Jesus is raised. Jesus participates in God's authority over all creation. He commissions his followers to worldwide mission, promising to be with them always. The economic, political, military and cultural power of Rome seemed absolute: Jesus was dead, Rome had won. But death was not the end: the alternative empire is one of death and resurrection, and death is defeated. Rome cannot resist God's alternative empire, and the message of Jesus' lordship over all humanity is to be spread throughout the world, as Jesus accompanies his followers to the ends of the earth.

Manifesto Of An Alternative Empire

Having outlined the broad shape of Matthew's Gospel as a whole, I will now focus on three particular chapters: the Sermon on the Mount. Scholars have spent generations discussing the purpose of the Sermon on the Mount, and it is unlikely that any one suggestion, least of all from me in a short book like this, will completely cover everything this great sermon does. But I suggest that one way of looking at the Sermon on the Mount is as a manifesto for an alternative empire, which sets out how people are to live in God's kingdom. Jesus knows we can never completely live up to this challenge, and his grace is available to all of us as we try, and fail, to respond to the demands of life in the alternative empire. I will first outline the shape of the sermon as a whole before concentrating on a specific passage that sets out one aspect of life in the alternative empire.

The setting is clear: Jesus is on a mountain, talking to his followers (5:1-2).[3] He begins by outlining the reward of being in the kingdom (5:3-12). Traditionally called the 'Beatitudes,'

---

[3] This overview is based on that found in Craig Keener. (1999). *A Commentary on the Gospel of Matthew*. Grand Rapids: Eerdmans, pp.160-257, supplemented with my own thoughts. The good bits are probably all Keener's ideas.

they set out the blessings of being in God's alternative empire and characterise the radically different values by which it operates. Next, using metaphors of salt and light, Jesus describes worthy and worthless disciples (5:13-16), before reminding his followers that they are expected to remain obedient to God's law (5:17-20). This obedience must not be literalist, or wooden, but from the heart, a radical whole-life change that is clearly visible to everyone, since the goal of the law is relationship with God, a goal that Jesus fulfills by his perfect obedience to the law.

Jesus then applies the principles of God's law (5:21-48), going to the heart of six controversial issues, reminding his disciples that the alternative empire is a place of whole-hearted devotion to God and love for humanity. In the alternative empire, we are not to be angry, because anger is a form of murder (5:21-26). We are not to covet others sexually, because it is a form of adultery (5:27-30). Nor are the married to betray their spouse through divorce, except in certain permitted circumstances (5:31-32). Jesus teaches that oaths are a poor substitute for integrity: we are to be people of our word who do not need to be held accountable by an oath (5:33-37). We are not to take revenge (5:38-42), but to love and pray for God's blessing on our enemies (5:38-48).

In the opening section of chapter six, Jesus teaches that we should show only God our righteousness, not acting to be noticed or applauded by others (6:1-18). He uses three examples; alms giving, prayer and fasting, but the principles apply to all acts of righteousness. The ethics of the alternative empire are not theory, but daily practice, rewarded by God for those who seek to impress God alone. The rest of chapter six teach about material possessions. Jesus' disciples are not to value possessions enough to seek them (6:19-24), but at the same time they are not to value possessions enough to worry about them (6:25-34). This teaching challenges both the poor, who want to get more, and the rich, who want to jealously hold on to what they have. Instead, we are to live only for the treasures of the alternative empire, the kingdom of heaven.

The alternative empire is not a place where we judge one another. Using humour and hyperbole, Jesus points out the stupidity of human beings judging one another (7:1-6). Rather than judging others, we are to seek to build up the alternative empire, asking God for the good gifts he longs to give us (7:7-12). The alternative empire is a difficult place to find and enter (7:13-14), and so only a few manage it. Many who claim to represent God are not citizens of the alternative empire, and their actions make this clear. They will be judged accordingly (7:15-23). Only those who truly obey Jesus' teachings will stand through the storms that rock the alternative empire, which is not always an easy place to be (7:24-27).

Eyes and love

I have picked the section on eyes and love (Matthew 5:38-48) because I think it is one passage that takes us to the heart of Matthew's presentation of the alternative empire. The text reads as follows:

> You have heard it said, "An eye for an eye and a tooth for a tooth," but I say to you, 'Do not resist an evil person; instead if someone strikes you on the right cheek, turn and offer him the other. And if someone wants to sue you, to take your tunic, give him your cloak as well. Whoever compels you to go with him one mile, go with him two. Give to whoever asks from you and don't turn away whoever wants to borrow from you.'

> You have heard it said, "Love your neighbour and hate your enemy," but I say to you, 'Love your enemy, and pray for those who persecute you, so that you may become sons of your father in heaven. He causes his sun

> *to rise on the evil and the good, and sends rain on the*
> *righteous and the unrighteous. What reward is there*
> *if you just love those who love you? Don't even the tax*
> *collectors do that? And if you greet only your brothers,*
> *what are you doing more than others? Don't even the*
> *pagans do that?'*
>
> *'You should be perfect, as your Father in heaven is*
> *perfect.'*

Matthew 5:38-48

Often we exaggerate to make a point. 'Don't touch that, you'll burn your hand off,' you might say to a toddler who wants to play with an open fire. In a similar way, Jesus uses hyperbole to challenge us about what we value and how we respond to others. The first paragraph is all about revenge. In Old Testament law, 'an eye for an eye and a tooth for a tooth' (Exodus 21:23-25; Deuteronomy 19:21) was a foundational legal principle, called *lex talionis*, which basically says the punishment should fit the crime. So if someone caused damage to another, such that they lost a tooth, then that is what they are to be compensated for. It is a way of limiting the desire for revenge, and ensuring that, in a society where honour was everything, attempts to expunge the humiliation of shame did not get out of hand.

Craig Keener suggests that striking the cheek was as much a challenge to someone's honour as a physical attack.[4] Jesus says, do not be so concerned for your own honour that you take revenge. Instead, leave justice in the hands of God. That same principle applies when someone tries to sue you for your tunic. Roman society was very litigious, and it was commonplace for wealthier people to make recourse to the courts. If Jesus' command were followed literally, then a poor peasant would become naked, loosing all their clothing,

---

[4] Craig Keener. (1999). *A Commentary on the Gospel of Matthew.* Grand Rapids: Eerdmans, pp.197-198.

a truly shameful situation in the society of the day. This makes me wonder if this is in fact a form of resistance, of radical non-violent direct action, whereby the one who is sued challenges the justice of the case by surrendering everything. Similarly, Roman soldiers had the right to force local peasants to carry their pack for one mile, but for the peasant to keep walking and carry it two would subvert the Roman authority structure, and potentially get the legionary in question into trouble for exploiting that privilege.

We have to think hard about how literally we should take these instructions. Jesus is clearly giving orders: the verbs are imperatives, telling the listener what to do. If we always did exactly what Jesus said here, would we soon be naked, penniless, homeless, bruised wrecks? Perhaps. Pastoral concerns make it difficult for me to be too directive, but most of us are so far away from coming close to actually doing what Jesus says here, that rather than explaining these instructions away, we should probably start to take them a bit more seriously.

The same could be said for the second paragraph, which is a radical call to love. The logic of Jesus' instructions is that God loves all of us and so we should love others. As Romans 5:8 reminds us, it was while we were still God's enemies that Christ died for us. It is while we were still God's enemies, that he sent the sun and the rain which cause crops to grow, which ensure we are fed and have enough to drink, that our basic needs are met. God does not discriminate in his general grace in providing for people, and so we who claim to follow him and live as citizens of his alternative empire should not hate anyone.

'Tax collectors' and 'pagans' are held up as examples of the least righteous of all people. But even they do good to those who are kind to them; even they greet one another. So, the logic of Jesus' argument runs, if even these unrighteous people are kind to those who have shown them kindness, then it is not unreasonable to expect a bit more of God's chosen people. We are to love, to pray for God's blessing on not just those we like or who are like us, but also for those whom we find awkward, annoying, troublesome or even hateful.

If you think about this carefully, then even this prayer of blessing is potentially a form of subversion, for what can be a greater blessing than a relationship with our Heavenly Father through his Son Jesus Christ in the power of his Spirit? This then is what we should pray for our enemies: that they are blessed by a living relationship with God, that they know his transforming power in their lives and that they too come to live as citizens of God's alternative empire. We should also pray for their material and emotional needs, as well as spiritual ones. And through praying for them, we can learn to love them as God loves them, and so draw them closer to his kingdom.

The section closes with Jesus' instruction that we are to be perfect, as our Father in heaven is perfect. This is not simply by flawless obedience to particular rules or laws, but through a complete righteousness of the heart, a total devotion to God's purposes in this world. It is the same instruction as that found in Leviticus: Be holy, as I am holy (Leviticus 11:44-45; 19:2; 20:26).

Questions

1. How seriously should we take Jesus' teaching about revenge? What would our lives actually look like if we tried to live this way?

2. How can we love our enemies? What about those who are annoying, irritating, or just hard to be with?

3. What enemies do you have and how can you put this teaching into practise in how you relate to them?

4. What does Jesus' command to be perfect make you think? How does it make you feel? How do you relate this command to your experience of God's grace?

Please Smite Him

"Father, everything within me wants to ask you to smite Terry with a lightning bolt and burn him to a crisp. But I know that is not what you would want me to pray, so through gritted teeth I ask you to bless him."

One of my more honest, even if not especially inspiring prayers. I can well remember praying it. I was standing in church, with the words of a song—I think it was *Guide me O Thou Great Redeemer*—coming out of my mouth. I wouldn't say I was singing it; certainly it was not coming out as a song of praise. But I was in church, everyone else was singing, and I would draw attention to myself if I did not also stand up and make the relevant noises. So there I was, the words duly coming out, while ever fibre of my being was concentrating on not walking across the aisle and punching Terry. I wanted to hit him. Not once, not even twice, but enough times to draw blood, to break some teeth.

Why are some people so hard to like?

Why are some people horrible towards you, whatever it is that you do?

I probably had not been as good to Terry as I could have been, but I would not say I was evil towards him. At least, I do not think I was. So how did we get to the point where all I really wanted to do was hit him and get God to smite him?

There has been a sort of rivalry between us for a very long time. We've both been coming to St Jude's for over twenty years. We have both been on the church council. We have both held leading roles: chair, secretary, church-warden, and all that sort of thing. Neither of us is any good at money; so neither of us has been treasurer. We even once both stood for warden, and since no one else did, we had to "work" together for a year. Longest year of my life. Happily he had done three years by then, so the vicar asked him to step down to allow someone else to have a go. I had two more years to go, so I stayed. Then when my three years were up, I had to stop as well, so it was not exactly a victory for me, but it felt good all the same.

During those twenty years at St Jude's there has not ever been one huge fight. It's more lots of little things. Angry words from him, talking behind my back, out-of-committee maneuvering so he's got his tanks parked on my lawn, and when I try and chair the meeting and encourage a free and open discussion, it's already been sewn up by his clique.

When someone fights dirty, I guess there is a bit of you that fights dirty back. That does your own pre-meeting meetings, canvasses for supporters, maybe talks the guy down a bit. And before you know it, you've got an enemy in church. Makes the peace before communion a bit of a challenge, I can tell you. Happily, at St Jude's the peace is a very English handshake with the three people closest to you before the organist starts the offertory hymn in a desperate bid to get home before the Sunday joint starts going dry and crispy. This meant I never had to shake hands with Terry, as we never sat anywhere near each other. But even so, it did bother me occasionally, but I never lost any sleep over it.

This grumbling, mutual animosity went on for at least a decade, but it came to a head three years ago. I know it was then, because the lectionary is a three year cycle, and we had the "love your enemies" reading from Matthew again this week. Time is a bit of a healer, but the burning anger in my gut is still there, even if it is only glowing embers that will roar back into full flame if I fuel them with the oxygen of hatred. I am doing my best to smother those embers with love, but it is hard.

Three years ago was St Jude's four-hundredth anniversary, a significant moment in the life of any congregation, and a catastrophic one for my relationship with Terry. I set my heart on a huge public event—a Saturday fun day on the August bank holiday weekend, with a free barbeque, bouncy castles for the kids, all that sort of thing. Sure, it was going to cost a bit of money, maybe three thousand quid to do it really well, but it would be such a great witness to the community, a chance to say that after four hundred years St Jude's was still alive and kicking.

Terry thought it was the worst idea possible. The absolute worst. And his PCC ambush shot it straight through the heart. A decision this big clearly should not be made in an evening by a group of tired commuters who really just want to go home and have a glass of whiskey before bed. But that's roughly how the Church of England works. And that was enough to put paid to it all. I had set out the idea in a meeting in January, and now having kicked it around a bit in February, we came to the decision point in March.

I was feeling good about it all. I thought I had been persuasive, people I talked to in church seemed positive and to like the idea. Yes, there was the issue of the boiler, but I did not foresee any problems at all.

I was wrong.

Never underestimate people's concern for their own comfort. St Jude's, a four hundred year old church, like many similar vintage buildings, has a very inadequate heating system. One that decided to become even more inadequate at the church reached its fourth centenary. So there were two big items on the agenda that evening—a new boiler and the centenary celebrations.

Terry likes to be warm. And he wanted a new boiler more than he wanted a free barbeque. He got what he wanted. The details of the meeting are too painful for me to recount in much detail, but at least four people, who I thought were my friends and supported me, each, in different ways, accused me of being indifferent to the needs of the elderly, arrogant, obsessed with taking the main stage, wanting to show off to outsiders rather than ensure that dedicated, faithful regular attenders did not freeze, as well as being cavalier with the church's money and refusing to listen to anyone. It got put to a vote, and I lost, badly. Prioritising fund raising for the boiler was carried with only one objection—mine.

I was gutted. Really cross. Terry sat looking smug, even came over after the end of the meeting, "to make sure I was okay" (that is, to twist the knife a bit more). Hand on my shoulder, sincere look of concern, "Are you alright? I hope that you're not upset about that little idea you had for a celebration on the green not happening are you? I'm sure there will be another opportunity."

I could have punched him.

Then the next Sunday, the lectionary reading was from Matthew. It was about asking God to bless your enemies, about praying for those who persecute you. Because we are a lectionary church, and it was the Gospel reading, I know Father Kenneth was not manipulating things. But he did look in my direction when he said, "And of course, our enemies may not be people trying to kill us. They may be people we have disagreements with in meetings or on the street. They may even be our irritating neighbours whose dog barks all night, keeping us awake."

I do not know if he meant it for me, but God did. So I prayed that prayer. Irritatingly, God seems to have answered it. He blessed Terry. We got the money for the boiler. We had a much smaller celebration on the August Bank Holiday Monday: a free barbeque, but no free bouncy castles or rides. About a hundred people came. It was okay. At least it did not rain.

I pray for Terry most weeks now. Just 'Lord, bless that irritating little man Terry.' It's all I can say, but I say it every Sunday, just after the peace, as the organ strikes up. I hate him less now. I no longer want to punch him. I have made progress in three years. Give it another three hundred, and I may even like him.

In this story I have tried to build on the fact that most of us do not really have enemies, at least not the sort of enemy who wants to kill us or do us serious harm. But most of us will have to spend time with people whom we find annoying: maybe a colleague at work, a neighbour or someone in church.

My experience is that of this story: I do find people annoying, and the only way I can learn to love them is to pray for God to bless them. Otherwise my sinful nature will encourage me to hate them or score points over them, precisely the opposite of what a Christian should do.

Chapter 4

Luke-Acts And Empire

Luke wrote two of the books in the New Testament: the Gospel that bears his name and also the Acts of the Apostles. It is common for scholars to talk about Luke-Acts as two volumes of one project in which Luke details what Jesus did when he was on earth, and then what he did through his Holy Spirit in growing the Early Church.

Another feature of Luke-Acts that is often noted is that one of his aims in writing was to explain to the Roman authorities that Christianity really was not a threat to them. Luke's attempt to persuade the Roman authorities not to worry about Christianity becomes very clear in the book of Acts, especially in the closing chapters, which document Paul's arrest in Jerusalem, and the efforts the Jewish authorities make to have him tried and condemned. Paul is a Roman citizen, and the Roman authorities cannot find a charge that sticks, so the book of Acts ends with Paul under house arrest in Rome, freely able to proclaim the good news of Jesus.

A Different Kind Of Empire

A lot of what is true of Matthew's Gospel is equally true of Luke's. Both of them share a vision of God's kingdom. But if it is true that Luke wrote to explain how Christianity was not a threat to Rome, how exactly does Luke-Acts set out the same alternative empire that Matthew and Mark do? I think Luke's aim was precisely to show that Jesus' alternative empire was not a political or military one, that it was inclusive of all, that it did not operate in the way the Roman Empire did, and so could not be thought of as a military or political rival.

At the start of Luke's Gospel, we are told three times who are the imperial rulers who dominate Israel. Moreover, three different authorities demand taxes: Rome itself, the Herodian kings and the tithes and offerings demanded of the priesthood (see Luke 1:5; 2:1-4; 3:1-2). Luke makes it clear that Jesus is born into a world dominated by a particular imperial power, a power that is subverted by a God who raises the humble and poor (as seen for example in Mary's song in Luke 1:46-55).[1]

Luke is very clear about the radical nature of God's kingdom, as a discussion of a few key passages will show. I'll begin by looking at one passage, which describes some of Jesus' followers:

> *After this Jesus travelled from one town and village to another, preaching and proclaiming the good news of the kingdom of God. The twelve were with him, together with some women whom had been cured of evil spirits and diseases; Mary, called Magdalene, from whom seven demons had come out; Joanna, the wife of Chuza, the manager of Herod's household; and Susanna, and*

[1] This theme is discussed at greater length in Brian J. Walsh and Sylvia C. Keesmaat. *Colossians re:mixed*, pp.69-71.

> *many others. These women were helping to support*
> *them from their own means.*

Luke 8:1-3

David W. Smith discusses the position of these women in some detail.[2] He notes that they follow Jesus from Galilee, and become witnesses to his death and resurrection (Luke 23:49; 24:10). The fact that they possess resources that they can use to support Jesus and his ministry indicates their own wealth, and suggests they were part of the urban elite. Smith notes that Mary's hometown of Magdala had become a prosperous fishing port, which salted and pickled fish for export across the Roman Empire. He adds that the spicy fish sauce called *garum* and fish stews known as *salsamentum* produced in Magdala became familiar to uban populations across the Roman Empire, so much so that the Jewish historian Josephus called the town *Tarichaeae*, a word signifying factories for the salting of fish. It seems likely, therefore, that Mary was a woman of means, an owner of a fish exporting business. Perhaps this is how she came to meet Joanna, the wife of Chuza, manager of Herod's household. It is impossible to know with any degree of certainty, but it is at least possible that this is the case. These are rich women, and they use their wealth to support Jesus, suggesting that the alternative empire has made inroads amongst those with money and power, as well as amongst the poor.

Another way of thinking about the difference between Rome's Empire and Jesus' Empire is their different understandings of glory. Both the Roman Empire and Jesus' alternative empire were interested in glory, but they understood it in very different terms. The Roman Emperors displayed their glory by big showy parades, by extravagant displays of wealth, by being noticed and by having power over people.

---

[2] David W. Smith. (2011). *Seeking A City With Foundations: Theology for an Urban World*. Nottingham: IVP, pp.181-183.

Jesus' glory is very different. Luke is clear that Jesus is the perfect manifestation of God's glory. But his glory is not what we might initially expect. It is not overbearing or dominant, but rather humble and self-sacrificial.

Thomas Martin suggests that in Luke's Gospel, Jesus' glory is primarily his humility. He suggests that Luke deliberately juxtaposes the two ideas of glory and humility. By glory, Martin means an emphasis on Jesus' royal exaltation as Lord of all Creation, reminding us that he is the one to whom all persons and all creation will bow. But glory is always linked with humility in Luke's Gospel, and as Martin reminds us, this means it acts as 'the counter-sign of all normal expectations for kings, princes, presidents, nations, multi-national corporations, pop-stars and splendidly robed bishops, well-dressed pastors, or famous church buildings.'[3] Jesus is glorious, but his glory is seen in his humility.

Martin suggests that the deliberate close association of glory and humility occurs throughout Luke's Gospel, notably in these places:

- Jesus is not accepted as a prophet by his own (Luke 4:23-30);

- Jesus deliberately chooses someone who would betray him to be in his most intimate circle. (Luke 6:16);

- Jesus teaches we should love our enemies (Luke 6:27-36);

- The Son of Man is accused of being a glutton and a drunkard (Luke 7:34);

- The glory of Jesus is shown in his humility as he is anointed by a sinful woman (Luke 7:36-50);

[3] Thomas W. Martin. (2006). What Makes Glory Glorious? Reading Luke's Account of the Transfiguration Over Against Triumphalism. *Journal for the Study of the New Testament* 29(1):3-26, page 5, footnote 7.

- He goes to the margins—foreigners, such as the centurion (Luke 7:1-10); women, such as raising the widow's son (Luke 7:11-17) and societal outcasts like Zacchaeus (Luke 19:1-10);

- In the transfiguration it is actually the humble Jesus, not the exalted Jesus, we are called to listen to (Luke 9:34);

- The triumphal entry is a further demonstration of glory through humility (Luke 19:28-44);

- Jesus' glory is even seen on the cross: one of the criminals who is crucified with him professes faith in Jesus and is welcomed into paradise (Luke 23:40-43) and the centurion who oversaw his execution recognises him as a righteous man (Luke 23:47).

The central themes of Luke's Gospel are that Jesus came to proclaim God's alternative empire, and that this empire is available to everyone, regardless of ethnicity, gender or social status. However, not everyone can be part of the alternative empire, which values the glory of humility, the inclusion of the marginalised and the love of enemies.

This Is Me, And This Is What I Stand For

Jesus sets out the values of his alternative empire in a passage that scholars have dubbed the 'Nazareth Manifesto' (Luke 4:14-30). Much like a political manifesto, in this passage Jesus sets out who he is and what he stands for. Luke 1-3 set up expectations of a conventional revolutionary messiah, someone chosen by God to bring in his kingdom. This might have led the first readers of Luke to expect Jesus to be a violent revolutionary, but such an understanding is overturned in

Luke 4 as the nature of God's kingdom is spelt out in more detail. In the first part of the chapter, Jesus is tempted by the devil. Having defeated him, he returns to his hometown:

Jesus returned to Galilee in the power of the Spirit. The report about him spread throughout the whole surrounding region. He taught in their synagogues, and everyone praised him.

He went to Nazareth, where he had been brought up. On the Sabbath day, as was his custom, he went to the synagogue and stood up to read. They gave him the scroll of the Prophet Isaiah, and he opened it to the place where it is written:

The Spirit of the Lord is on me, because he has anointed me to preach the good news to the poor. He has sent me to proclaim freedom to the prisoners and sight to the blind, to send freedom for the oppressed and to proclaim the year of the Lord's favour.

He closed up the scroll, gave it back to the attendant and sat down. Everyone in the synagogue fastened their eyes on him. He began by saying to them, "Today, this scripture was fulfilled in your hearing."

Everyone witnessed him, and were amazed at the gracious words he spoke. They asked, "Isn't this Joseph's son?"

Jesus replied, "Surely you will quote this proverb at me, 'Doctor, heal yourself.' Why don't you do here in your hometown the things we heard you did in Capernaum?"

"I tell you the truth," he continued, "No prophet is accepted in his hometown. As you truly know, there were many widows in Israel in Elijah's day, when the sky was shut for three years and six months, and there was a terrible famine in the land. But Elijah was not sent to any of them, but to a widow of Zarephath in the region

*of Sidon. And there were many lepers in Israel when
Elisha was prophet, but none of them were cleansed,
only Naaman the Syrian."*

*Everyone in the synagogue was furious when they
heard this. They got up, drove him out of the town, and
up onto the brow of the hill on which the town was built,
to throw him off. But he passed through the crowd and
went on his way.*

Luke 4:14-30

This is Luke's account of Jesus' manifesto for the alternative empire. It was not well received by many who heard it.
Jesus begins by quoting from Isaiah 61, which was a popular
liberation text. But he also associated it with Isaiah 58, making it clear that his ministry would be focused on sacrifice
and care for the marginalised. Jesus also left out the promise
of vengeance that is found in Isaiah 61:2, and so removed all
reference to hostility towards the Gentiles. The congregation
who hear are thus amazed that Jesus preaches a message of
grace, that does not involve revenge on the Gentiles. They understand he has widened the scope of the message of Isaiah
61 to include those they themselves reject and despise, and
so they choose to also reject Jesus.

The reaction of the crowd in 4:22 is uncertain. I have used
'everyone witnessed him,' to try and capture the ambiguity
of Luke's phrase. I. Howard Marshall explains that the word
variously means 'to bear witness to' with a positive connota-
tion, or 'to bear witness against' or 'to condemn' in a negative
sense.[4] Jesus' next words reveal that the people were either
jealous of the signs Jesus performed elsewhere and thought
they had the right to see signs because Nazareth is Jesus'
hometown or that 'Jesus should provide signs to attest the

[4] I. Howard Marshall. (1978). *The Gospel of Luke: A Commentary on the Greek Text.*
Carlisle: Paternoster, p.185.

verbal claims which he has made.'[5] Jesus' further comments about how God's kingdom reaches out beyond ethnic Israel enrage the crowd, and they try to throw him down the cliff as the first stage of attempting to stone him to death for blasphemy (4:29-30).

In this passage, Jesus proclaims an agenda that focuses on the poor, the captives, the blind and the oppressed. To them he proclaims good news, liberty, sight, and "the year of the Lord's favour". In summary, Jesus claims that he will bring salvation to the lowly, much as Mary, Zechariah, and Anna's songs proclaim at the start of Luke (1:46-55, 68-79; 2:29-32). This is the nature of the alternative empire, where all are welcomed regardless of their gender, ethnicity or social status.

Joel Green suggests that the emphasis on release, in Jesus' words, together with the final appeal to 'the year of the Lord's favour,' links the Nazareth Manifesto not only to Isaiah 58:6; 61:1-2, but, more deeply, to legislation related to the Jubilee in Leviticus 25.[6] In the Year of Jubilee, Israel must

> proclaim liberty throughout the land to all its inhabitants. It shall be a jubilee for you, when each of you shall return to his property and each of you shall return to his clan. That fiftieth year shall be a jubilee for you; in it you shall neither sow nor reap.... It shall be holy to you.
>
> Leviticus 25:10-12

Further, God promises to provide food for the year (25:21-22). No one is to wrong another when selling or buying (25:17). All property will be released to its former owner (25:23-28). Scholar Howard Yoder connects the Year of Jubilee to Luke's 'the year of the Lord's favour' and describes Jubilee

[5] Marshall, *The Gospel of Luke*, p.187.
[6] Joel B. Green. (1995). *The Theology of the Gospel of Luke*. Cambridge: Cambridge University Press, p.78.

as 'the time when the inequities accumulated through the
years are to be crossed off and all God's people will begin
again at the same point.'[7]

Although at first glance it seems that release from debt,
rest and kindness toward the poor is the primary focus of
Leviticus 25, we must remember that the intention of the
Year of Jubilee law, as with the Sabbath law, is first and
foremost theological and spiritual and a symbol of the relationship between God and his people. For example, Leviticus
25:17 connects doing good to one another in keeping with
the Jubilee law and with the fear of God. Leviticus 25:23-24
commands the redemption of property on the basis that the
land is God's and Israel are 'strangers and sojourners' with
God. Leviticus 25:38, 42-43, 55 further bases relationships
to the poor on Israel's status as redeemed servants of God,
whom he 'brought out of the land of Egypt.' Because all God's
people are redeemed slaves, they must treat their brothers
and sisters with kindness.

There are echoes of all these ideas from Leviticus in Jesus'
speech at Nazareth. Thus, Jesus sets out the basis of the alternative empire in continuity with the kingdom that God has
begun to bring into the world through the people of Israel,
and now extends to the whole world.

A second passage, which adds further emphasis to my
argument, is the account of the transfiguration. In Luke 9,
Jesus sends out the Twelve, to preach the good news of the
kingdom, heal the sick and drive out demons. They return to
him when they have done so, and Jesus tries to take them
away to a quiet place. Unfortunately a huge crowd follows,
and Jesus ends up feeding them all with one boy's meal of
five small barley loaves and two fish. Having fed the crowd,
they are dismissed and Jesus asks his close followers whom
the crowds say he is, and then whom they think he is. Peter
answers that Jesus is 'The Christ of God' (Luke 9:20). He is

[7] John H. Yoder. (1994). *The Politics of Jesus.* Grand Rapids: Eerdmans, p.29.

warned not to tell this to anyone, and also that the Christ would suffer much, would be killed in Jerusalem and after three days raised to life.

> *About eight days after Jesus had said this, he took Peter and John and James and went up a mountain to pray. While he was praying, the appearance of his face changed and his clothes became as white as a flash of lightning. Two men talked with him, who were Moses and Elijah. They appeared in glorious splendour and talked of his exodus, which he was about to fulfill in Jerusalem. Peter and his companions were very tired, but when they awoke they saw his glory and that of the two men standing with him. As the men were leaving Jesus, Peter said to him, "Master, it is good for us to be here. Let us put up three tents: one for you, one for Moses and one for Elijah." He did not know what he was saying.*
>
> *While he was speaking, a cloud covered them and they were terrified as they entered the cloud. A voice came from the cloud, "This is my Son, whom I have chosen. Listen to him." When the voice had spoken, they found Jesus alone. The disciples kept this to themselves and did not tell anyone at the time what they had seen.*
>
> Luke 9:28-36

As the moment when Jesus reveals his glory to his closest followers, the transfiguration is something of an anticlimax. Only three people see it, and they are so terrified by what they have seen, they do not tell anyone else. This is not a triumphant emperor coming at the end of a vast procession in front of an adoring crowd. It's three terrified blokes in a cloud who have no real idea what is going on. That is glory linked with humility.

Moreover, as Thomas Martin notes, Jesus' true glory is not shown when his face changes and his clothes become white like lightning. Instead, his true glory is hidden in the dark mysterious cloud out of which comes the voice of God. And when Jesus emerges from the cloud he is alone and very normal. This is the Jesus that God commands us to listen to.[8]

The point is underlined by what happens when they go down the mountain the next day. The crowd surround Jesus, and he has to heal a boy who is tormented by a demon, and it seems the crowd are not even sure if Jesus can do this (Luke 9:37-43). Then Jesus teaches again that he will suffer and die (Luke 9:44-45) and they respond by arguing about which one of them is the greatest (Luke 9:46-48). This is not the glory of an emperor, but the humble glory of the alternative empire.

Questions

1. What does Jesus' Nazareth Manifesto teach us? If we want to follow Jesus, how should it impact how we live?

2. In Luke 4, Jesus teaches that God's alternative empire welcomes everyone, regardless of gender, ethnicity or social status. How true is that of our church and our daily lives?

3. In Luke 4, Jesus upset many people by his teaching. Does how we live our Christian lives upset others?

4. I suggested in Luke 9 that Jesus' glory is seen in his humility. What do you think this sort of glorious humility looks like in daily life? How do we avoid becoming a doormat but also avoid being arrogant?

5. What encounters have you had with Jesus that have really challenged and changed you?

[8] Martin. 'What Makes Glory Glorious?', p.22.

You Are Welcome, Really You Are

'So this is a banana,' I said, continuing my slide into abject failure as a host. Nakamura stared at me, his face a mask. 'I don't suppose you have them in Japan,' I continued. 'They taste quite nice. English people love them. We normally open them at the top, here.' I demonstrated. 'My cousin says you should open them at the other end, but I think that's quite wrong.'

Nakamura smiled slightly. 'I didn't know bananas were native to the UK,' he quietly corrected me. 'In Japan, ours normally come from Costa Rica, but sometimes from the Caribbean as well. On weekends, people from my church often buy them by the box-load, and we take them to the homeless when they gather at the back of the malls.'

Realisation of my own idiocy opened a chasm beneath me. Sadly, it was only metaphorical, not the literal hole I wanted at that moment. I stuttered my apology, and thanked him for his gracious reply.

I really enjoyed having Nakamura stay for those three weeks. His English was impressive. Of course, he had an accent, and was occasionally slightly lost for words. But all I could say in Japanese was *ohayo* to greet him in the morning and *arigato* to express my gratitude when he bought me a coffee or paid for lunch, as happened quite often during those few weeks.

He was supposed to be learning from me, doing a three-week stint of homestay in an average English home, attending an average English church. Nakamura is the pastor of a small evangelical church in Osaka, one of Japan's bigger cities. The church itself was planted in the early 1950s, as part of MacArthur's drive to 'Christianise' Japan, to ensure war never happened again. It sort of worked. Churches were established, but none grew very big, and most of Japan is indifferent to the call of Jesus Christ to 'Come, follow me.'

In recent years, economic stagnation and weariness with the rat race and dissolution with materialism has meant a few more seekers. But it has also meant a rise in right-wing nationalism, and it was this Nakamura was studying. He wanted to get behind the secenes, to understand how the far right was on the rise in Britain and what he could take and apply in Japan. Unfortunately all he got was three weeks staying with an idiot like me who patronised him about bananas during the first lunch we shared together.

Happily, although I made a few other mistakes, they were all taken in good humour. Nakamura ate impressive quantities of rice, his staple of choice. I did not really appreciate how important it was to him. I kept offering bread, pasta and potatoes as alternatives for variety, but he really preferred rice three meals a day. Providing him with what he preferred for washing was a challenge too. Apparently a long, hot soak in a tub is what every Japanese really likes. Nakamura showered when with us, but a week into his stay, he was showing us pictures of his home and we realised we were letting him down on the ablutions front. The idea of sharing a bath with my entire family (using the water in turn, not all at once), was something that made me shiver slightly in disgust, even after he explained that everyone washes thoroughly first. Once he had explained, we gladly let him have his hour long baths, but only in the evening and only once we'd all been to the loo first.

These wrinkles were the normal bumps to be ironed out in any visit, and they were never really a problem. Like I said, Nakamura came to learn, and he had that generosity and open heart which made having him with us such a joy. We shared so many concerns. Both of us did some work with the homeless, mainly chatting with individuals, encouraging them not to give up on Jesus, even if the church did seem to have largely given up on them. Both of us noticed a growth in extremist rhetoric, fostering a spirit of 'everyone for themselves,' which we both thought the direct opposite of Jesus' command to 'love others as yourself.' Sadly both of us were not really sure how to counter this.

'The thing is,' Nakamura gestured with his water glass at another of our lunchtime chats, 'the stories they tell are so much more attractive. Tales of the glory days, accounts of how foreigners hurt Japan and continue to hurt her, messages of how we must just work more, build up the army, make the nation great. A story people want to hear.'

He paused in his tales of Japan's right wing to slurp some noodles. I was impressed with myself for finding this Ramen bar for him, but even more impressed by the noise he made eating the noodles in their soup. Apparently it was good manners and showed enjoyment. My kids loved hearing about that, although their mum was not so sure.

'And what can I offer as an alternative?' he went on. 'Come and sit for an hour a week on the one day you have free, come and sit with eight old women, two of whom hate each other for reasons I cannot understand. Come into a slightly cold concrete building that has seen better days. Come and read a book written in dated Japanese. If you're fortunate, come and sit with the two families who come to church when they can, but are often too busy or tired. How do we share our hope?'

Nakamura gazed at me for a moment, passion shining in his deep brown eyes. He bent his head to slurp more noodles, giving me a moment to recover from the blunt language of a non-native speaker and try to think of an answer.

I didn't have one, though I longed for one.

I sighed.

60

'I ask myself the same question, normally in the depths of winter in a gloomy, freezing cold, virtually empty church,' I sympathised. 'The thing I keep holding on to is the faithfulness and hospitality of God. He knows what we are struggling with. He is aware of our limited abilities, our lack of resources. He knows we are trying, but most people are just not at all interested. And he is faithful to those who remain faithful to him. He welcomes and feeds every one of us at his table, regardless of who we are or what we have done. And one by one he calls his people to himself. All I can do is pray with all my soul, serve with all my strength, love him and his world with all my heart and leave the rest to him.'

Like many stories, although this short piece is a work of fiction, it is based in fact. When I was at secondary school, I did once explain how to peel a banana to a Japanese boy who was home-staying with us. Happily my mother pointed out to me how stupid I was being, and I was (hopefully) a much better host after that.

This story tries to bring out some of the challenges of hospitality, especially when our guest comes from a completely different culture from our own, and has lots of assumptions that we do not share. It also touches on the challenges of proclaiming the good news of Jesus: liberation, sight, healing, freedom, forgiveness, peace, all that and more, to a world that is somewhat indifferent.

Chapter 5

John and Empire

In John's Gospel, Jesus is no friend of Rome. This is clear in many places, not least in his arrest and subsequent trial. Jesus is blunt in his statement to Pontius Pilate, the Roman Governor, when he tells him that his kingdom is not of this world (John 18:36). Jesus goes on to draw a contrast between human kingdoms, whose servants fight to protect their ruler, and his kingdom, which is completely different. Jesus has brought God's alternative empire close to the world, in order that the world can see what they are missing. Sadly, John's Gospel teaches us that, because human beings love darkness and act badly, they shun God's kingdom and remain in their own little empires.

Not Of This World

The presence of God's alternative empire is seen throughout John's Gospel. John begins with the very beginning, the presence of the Word with God, the one through whom creation came into being. The Word took human form, lived among us, and his first followers witnessed his glory, as he came, full of grace and truth, to speak of God's kingdom. John's Gospel is normally divided up into four parts: the prologue (chapter 1), Jesus' public ministry (chapters 2 to 12), his farewell conversation with his disciples, passion and resurrection (chapters 13 to 20) and an epilogue (chapter 21).[1]

As with the other Gospels, in John Jesus makes clear statements of his own identity and performs miracles that demonstrate he is whom he claims to be. He shows us he is God, and so the leader of the alternative empire. In John's Gospel, this is especially clear in the 'I am' sayings, which echo God's self-disclosure to Moses in Exodus.[2] Moses has seen the burning bush, and is talking with God. Moses has been told to go to the people of Israel, and tell them that God will deliver them. But Moses is unsure about the task, and seeks further reassurance:

> Moses said to God, 'Suppose I go to the Israelites and say to them, "The God of your fathers has sent me to you," and they ask me, "What is his name?" Then what shall I tell them?'
>
> God said to Moses, 'I am who I am. This is what you are to say to the Israelites: "I am has sent me to you."'

Exodus 3:13-14

Jesus uses this same 'I am' to describe himself in John's Gospel, clearly equating himself with God. The phrase occurs lots of times, each one echoing the divine name: 'the bread of life' (6:35, 48; see also 6:51); 'the light of the world' (8:12; cf. 12:46); 'the sheep's door' (10:7; 'the door' in 10:9); 'the good

---

[1] Stephen Smalley. (1998). *John: Evangelist and Interpreter.* Carlisle: Paternoster, pp.142-153.

[2] Warren Carter. (2006). *John: Storyteller, Interpreter, Evangelist.* Peabody: Hendrikson, pp.122-126.

shepherd" (10:11, 14); 'the resurrection and the life' (11:25); 'the way and the truth and the life' (14:6); and 'the true vine' (15:1; cf. 15:5 'the vine'). There are also five occasions where Jesus simply identifies himself as 'I am' (6:20; 8:28, 58; 13:9; 18:5), although these are not always clear in English translations. By using God's name to refer to himself, Jesus is clear that he is not simply a human being, and that his kingdom is not of this world.

As well as using God's name as his own, Jesus also performs miracles that show his divine power. The key miracles are: turning water into wine (2:1-11); the healing of the Official's son (4:43-53); the healing at the pool (5:1-15); the feeding miracle (6:1-15); walking on water (6:16-21); the healing of the man born blind (9:1-12); and the raising of Lazarus (11:1-44). Jesus shows that he has power over nature, the ability to heal with a word, mastery of death and that he brings life in all its fullness. The massively generous provision of wine at the wedding at Cana shows his kingdom to be full of life and joy; the healing miracles reinforce this, as does the abundant provision when thousands are fed. Even death has no place in this alternative empire, as Lazarus is raised from death and returned to his sisters, as a foretaste of Jesus' own victory over death.

Jesus' empire is not like any human empires, and those who encounter him struggle to understand exactly what it is he stands for. Thus, for example, Nicodemus comes at night to talk with Jesus (3:1-21), but does not really grasp whom he is. The low-status poor, lacking power, honour and resources, such as the man who had been sick for thirty-eight years (5:1-9) or the man born blind (9:1-8) are healed and restored. A child (4:46-54), a Samaritan woman (chapter 4) and low status Galileans (chapter 6) are all caught up in God's purposes, while the rich and powerful fail to understand.[3] The alternative empire is real and powerfully present, but many

[3] Carter, *John: Storyteller, Interpreter, Evangelist*, p.172.

respond negatively, just as John said they would (John 1:10-11).

A particularly striking feature of John's Gospel is the long dinner-table conversation Jesus has with his followers, on the night before he died. It is often called the 'Farewell Discourse' and is Jesus' goodbye to his followers (John 13:1-17:26). The overarching theme of this section is 'do not let your hearts be troubled' (14:1). Jesus prepares his disciples to deal with the fear and loneliness they are facing as a result of his immanent departure, and prepares them to live with each other in the world after he has gone. It is at this juncture that he gives them the supreme commandment that enjoins mutual love and warns them of the world's hatred:

> A new command I give you: love one another. As I have loved you, so you must love one another. By this everyone will know that you are my disciples, if you love one another. ... My command is this: love each other as I have loved you. Greater love has no-one than this: to lay down one's life for one's friends.
>
> John 13:34-35; 15:12-13

The alternative empire is characterised by love for others, in particular by love for fellow Christians.[4] This love is not simply an emotion, but practical action, which Jesus demonstrates by washing his disciples' feet. Jesus has been bringing this empire in throughout his ministry. Another key feature of the alternative empire that is covered in this section is the role of the Holy Spirit, whom Jesus calls the Comforter or Advocate, the one who comes alongside the disciples to help them follow Jesus. Right at the end of the farewell discourse, Jesus prays for his followers, a prayer which sets out his

---

[4] D. Moody Smith. (1995). *New Testament Theology: The Theology of the Gospel of John.* Cambridge: Cambridge University Press, pp.146-149.

vision for how they are to live in the world but not be part of the world. I will look at this text in more detail below.

Another notable feature of John's Gospel is the fact that Jesus is fully in control of his own destiny; he is one who chooses his own fate in obedience to God. As Warren Carter notes, Rome crucified those who opposed her or threatened her power.[5] But Jesus is in control of what happens to himself. His arrest in John 18:6 sets the tone very clearly. Judas and the soldiers come to the garden to arrest Jesus. Jesus asks them whom they want, and they reply 'Jesus of Nazareth.' 'I am he,' Jesus replies. When Jesus said, 'I am he,' they drew back and fell to the ground. The alternative empire may not be part of the world, but that does not mean the world has any power over it.

Jesus remains in control of his death. He arranges for his mother to be cared for, while nailed to the cross. To fulfil the scriptures, he says that he is thirsty. Having chosen his own death, Jesus dies to complete the work that the Father has given him, crying 'it is finished' (19:30). Jesus' death is his glorification; he is then raised in triumph, and returns to the Father. Jesus remains in control even after his death: his bones are not broken, in accordance with the Scriptures. And his resurrection shows that the worst that Rome can do, putting to death the revealer and agent of God's purposes in the world, cannot frustrate God's purposes, as God raises him from the dead.

Jesus makes a number of resurrection appearances: first to Mary Magdalene, then to all the disciples apart from Thomas; then to Thomas together with the other disciples. In this last appearance, Thomas recognises Jesus as 'my Lord and my God' (20:28). The Gospel finishes with the forgiveness of Peter and some hints as to who wrote the Gospel, and his role in the early church. It is significant that Peter is forgiven

[5] Carter, *John: Storyteller, Interpreter, Evangelist*, p.171.

by Jesus: the alternative empire is characterised by grace, by a second chance for those who admit their failures.

Jesus comes to bring in God's alternative empire, and also to judge the empire of this world. Rome's world is under judgement. Jesus is the truth and he had established a community that participates in a very different reality, namely the very life of God (John 5:24; 17:3). His community is 'commissioned to do the works Jesus did (14:12-17), to reveal God's life-giving purposes even though it will be tough and resisted work (15:18-25).[6]

Jesus Prays For Us

I'm not especially good at praying, and so find it really encouraging to know that Jesus prayed for, and continues to pray for, me. John 17 records a particularly detailed prayer of Jesus for the whole church, which reminds us of our calling to be fully involved with, yet completely distinct from, the society in which we find ourselves.

> After Jesus said this, he lifted up his eyes to heaven and said. 'Father, the hour has come: glorify your Son, so that your Son can glorify you. For you have given him authority over everyone, so that he can give eternal life to those whom you have given him. And this is eternal life: to know you, the only true God, and Jesus Christ, whom you have sent. I have glorified you on earth by finishing the work you gave me to do. So Father, now glorify me in your presence with the glory which I had from you since before the world began.
>
> 'I have revealed your name to those whom you gave me out of the world. They were yours and you gave them

[6] Carter, *John: Storyteller, Interpreter, Evangelist*, p.172.

to me and they obeyed your word. Now they know that everything you have given me comes from you, for I gave them the words you gave me and they accepted them. They truly know that I came from you and they believed that you sent me.

'I pray for them. I do not pray for the world, but for those whom you gave me, for they are yours. All I have is yours and all you have is mine, and I am glorified by them. I am no longer in the world, but they are in the world, and I am coming to you. Holy Father, protect them by the power of your name, the name which you have given me, so that they may be one as we are one. When I was with them, I protected them and kept them safe by the name which you have given me, and none of them was lost, except for the son of destruction, so that the Scripture might be fulfilled.

'I am coming to you now, but I say these things while I am still in the world, so that they might have the fulness of my joy within them. I have given them your word, and the world has hated them, because they are not of the world, just as I am not of the world. I am not praying that you will take them out of the world, but that you will keep them safe from the evil one. They are not of the world, just as I am not of the world. Sanctify them in truth; your word is truth. Just as you sent me into the world, so I am sending them into the world. I sanctify myself for them, so that they may be truly sanctified.

'I do not pray for them alone, but also for those who will believe because of what they say about me, that they may be one, just as you are in me Father and I am in you, so that they may also be in us, and the world may believe that you sent me. I have given them the glory which you gave me, so that they can be one just as we are one; I in them and you in me, so that all may be completely one, and the world will know that you sent me and love them just as you love me.

69

> *'Father, I want those whom you have given me to be*
> *with me where I am, to see my glory, the glory which*
> *you have given me because you loved me from the*
> *foundation of the world. Righteous Father, the world*
> *does not know you, but I know you, and they know that*
> *you sent me; I have made your name known to them,*
> *and will continue to make you known, so that the love*
> *which you have for me may be in them, and I may be in*
> *them.'*

John 17:1-26

There are a number of themes running through this prayer that I think it is important for us to notice.

First, there is the idea of glory, which is found throughout John's Gospel. Jesus is glorified by his Father, and reveals his Father's glory. What is striking is that, just as in Luke's Gospel, glory is not about power over people, but about service of them: Jesus' glory is revealed supremely when he is nailed to a cross, naked and in agony, suffering to win us freedom, forgiveness and redemption from shame and failure. The glory of humility, of self-giving in the service of others is at the heart of John's understanding of Jesus' alternative empire.

Second, notice the intimacy between Jesus and his Father, an intimacy which we are invited to share. The alternative empire is founded on that close relationship between the Father and the Son, and we become fellow-children with Jesus of our Father in Heaven. The Father gives us to Jesus who cares for us, and we are expected to be obedient to the Father's teachings. The idea of Jesus being sent by the Father as the main herald and messenger of the good news of the alternative empire is strongly present in this section. If we chose to follow Jesus, we are caught up in that most intimate of relationships between the Father and the Son, and through doing so, bring greater glory to the Son.

Third, the security of that relationship is eternal and unbreakable. Jesus protects those whom the Father has given him by the power of the Father's name. In this context, 'name' signifies 'everything about God.' So when Jesus says he has revealed the Father's name to his followers, he means he has revealed God to them, and when he says he has protected them by the power of the Father's name, he means that the Father's very being protects them. And everyone is protected, except for Judas, the 'son of destruction,' whose betrayal of Jesus was foretold in the Scriptures.

Fourth, Jesus wants us to be filled with joy: he tells us that he is praying for us, so that we might have the full measure of his joy within us, knowing that the one who spoke creation into being is concerned for our welfare. We need Jesus' joy because we are hated by the world. John is very clear that membership of the alternative empire means hatred from the world; he talks in black-and-white language, leaving no space for gray. Being in Jesus does not mean being hidden either; we are protected but not concealed. We are clearly visible in the world, separated from it (for that is what sanctified, or set apart, means), but involved with it, transforming the empires of the world from within, winning people and societies for the alternative empire of God's kingdom.

Fifth, did you spot the penultimate paragraph, where Jesus prays for us, those who have believed because of what other people told them about Jesus? He is concerned for our welfare, and spells out the intimacy of the relationship between the Father, the Son and the followers of Jesus. The detail of who is in whom may be confusing, but the main point is clear: we are included in that most intimate of relationships if we choose to be. The goal of this unity is the revelation of the glory of God and knowledge of the Father's love; unity for witness and for the salvation of all who trust in Christ.

Questions

1. John expects Jesus' alternative empire to be characterised by love. What does this look like in practical terms?

2. What do you find particularly striking about Jesus' prayer in John 17?

3. How can we live lives filled with joy in God's alternative empire?

4. What is your understanding of the close relationship between the Father and the Son, and how does it impact you personally?

United In Prayer

I honestly cannot think of another place where I would spend anything like this much time with this group of people, I really cannot. I mean, I work in a bank. Why would I spend a few hours a week with a long distance lorry driver and a stay-at-home mum, an Afghan refugee, a Spanish nurse and two Goths? But these people all come round to my house every week on a Thursday evening, and we talk about stuff that is important to us, the problems we are facing, and what the Bible has to say to our situation. It is the beauty of God's people; we are all so very different, but united around Jesus. Sure, we get on each other's nerves, we argue about politics or football or food. But we are a family, in a weird and wonderful kind of a way. And there is something precious about our meeting together.

The most powerful times are when we pray. Ahmed is much more comfortable praying in Pashto than praying in English. He became a Christian while still living in

Afghanistan, as an indirect result of working as an interpreter for the British army. He came to the UK because of fear of reprisals due to his work, and did not talk to anyone about his faith before he just walked into church one Sunday and asked to be baptised.

Antonia is also much happier praying in Spanish rather than in English. She does not talk very much, and only rarely prays out loud. But when she does there's so much passion in the few quietly murmured sentences that you can sense an intimacy with Jesus I wish I shared. I imagine she's a great nurse. I have never seen her in action, but her warmth of character, and concern for everyone's welfare speak volumes. I mean, it's my house we meet in, but she's the one taking the time to ensure everyone is comfy, has the drink they want, and so on.

Sally is always glad of the chance to talk. Spending her days caring for George, their one-year-old, means she's sometimes starved of adult conversation, so any talking is good. Her husband is always in on a Thursday night, and she comes to us for some God time. Very occasionally her prayers have a word or two of baby talk, which never fails to make me smile. Her tendency to use baby sign language, palm of the hand moved forward from the mouth for thank you, is really touching. It's one I've started doing myself, especially when its not appropriate to speak aloud. A quick gesture with your hand, further down from the mouth to say 'Please God help,' as I enter a potentially stressful situation and the smaller gesture for 'thank you' afterwards does wonders for my nerves.

Tony is our other talker. When conversation heads into one of those tumbleweed moments, you can guarantee that in less than ten seconds either Tony or Sally will have a contribution. Like Sally, Tony is often away from adults, although in his case it is because he drives his lorry alone. His firm specialises in transporting bulk goods, so as often as not he is driving load after load of soil or coal or metal ore from a building site or railway depot to some nearby destination. Skilled work in a sense, but crushingly dull in another, from Tony's point of view the main advantage is he nearly always gets to sleep in his own bed, much better than other driving jobs he's had. And his logistics controller normally gets him home on a Thursday in time to join us. Tony is a real prayer warrior. 'I often talk to Jesus in me cab,' he told us once. 'Keeps me company. We talk about all sorts of stuff, from West Ham's form in the Premiership to the spread of Ebola throughout West Africa. There's always lots to discuss and there's no one to tell me I'm mad, although I guess some of you might,' he finished with a grin.

Chris and Chris, our two Goths, are far chattier than you might expect. A married couple who share the same abbreviated name (Christine and Christopher on the marriage certificate), the first evening with them shattered my preconception and made me ashamed of my prejudices. They have a dress sense that baffles me, a liking for white face and dark eyes to make any panda proud and there is not a single piece of music that both they and I like. But none of that really matters. They love Jesus and so do I. Their prayers are short and direct, whether thanking, praising or asking, it's invariably a sentence, two at the most. But just like a child to her dad, it gets the point across and nobody is in any doubt as to what was meant.

There is something really special about the end of our Bible study. As often as not we ramble off topic, argue about exactly what it might mean and do not necessarily reach any firm conclusion. But once we have started sharing our needs and then we get round to praying, it is as though we are all joined together with Jesus holding us all close.

In this story I have tried to capture the reality of a church small group, where a diverse group of people, whose only real thing in common is a love for Jesus Christ, meet together, and most importantly, pray together. Both set words and extemporary prayers are equally important, both have riches, and both can be abused. What this story suggests is that whatever divides us, prayer unites us.

Chapter 6

Paul and Empire

The Apostle Paul appears, at least on a superficial reading of his letters and the book of Acts, to have had an ambiguous relationship with the Roman Empire. On the one hand, Paul clearly benefitted from some of the privileges of empire. Paul was a Roman citizen and he was not above using that fact to his own advantage. This is especially clear in his appeals to the protection that his status as a Roman citizen gave him (see Acts 16; 22 for two examples of this). Paul also talks in Romans 13 about the need to obey the authorities. On the other hand, the book of Acts ends with Paul under house arrest, and at least one of his letters (Philippians) makes it clear that he is in prison for his faith. Elsewhere in his letters he is clear that worship is due to God alone, and any worship of idols is false and abhorrent. How is it possible for the same man to experience both protection and imprisonment from the Roman authorities?

Paul the Roman citizen

When Paul describes his credentials to the Philippian church, he talks only of his Jewish pedigree: circumcised on the eight day, in strict obedience to the Law of Moses; a member of Benjamin's tribe, with clear Israelite lineage; a Pharisee who was not above persecuting the church for their heresy before he met Jesus on the road to Damascus (Philippians 3:5-6). Elsewhere in the same letter, he tells them that those 'who belong to Caesar's household' (4:22) remember them, and he begins the letter by talking about how the 'whole palace guard' are aware of why he is 'in chains' (1:13-14). The most likely explanation is that he is under arrest in Rome, possibly close to, or in, the imperial palace.[1] In other words, Paul's adherence to the Christian faith has meant that he has incurred the full wrath of Rome. He is a citizen of the alternative empire, and is paying the price for that obedience.

Paul's letter to the Philippians is, when read carefully, full of anti-imperial messages. The section that exalts Jesus is a clear challenge to any understanding of a Roman emperor as a god. Paul is encouraging the Philippian Christians to care for and support each other, and he writes:

> *Have amongst yourselves the same mindset that was also in Christ Jesus, who though he had the nature of God, did not consider equality with God something to be grasped, but emptied himself, taking the nature of a slave, being born in human likeness, and being found in appearance as a human being, humbled himself, being obedient to death, the death of a cross. Therefore, God has exalted him and given him the name that is above every name, so that at the name of Jesus every knee will bow, whether on heaven or on earth or under the earth,*

---

[1] Peter T. O'Brien. (1991). *New International Greek Testament Commentary: The Epistle to the Philippians.* Carlisle: Paternoster, pp.92-94.

> *and every tongue confess that Jesus Christ is Lord to the*
> *glory of God the Father.*

Philippians 2:5-11

Every knee will bow before Jesus, not before the emperor. Jesus is God come down among us, God in human flesh, fully divine yet also fully human. Jesus is Lord, writes Paul, yet in the Roman empire of his day, as James Harrison notes, from the time of Augustus onwards, the title 'Lord' was transferred as an honorific from the eastern ruler cult to the imperial cult. 'So thoroughly had the Julian-Claudians eclipsed their political rivals that talk of 'another Lord,' without any deference to or incorporation into their power base, was inconceivable.'[2] Yet Paul subverts this view in his hymn of praise to Jesus.

The same subversion of empire can be found in Paul's letter to the Colossians. There is a passage in that letter which also sets out Paul's understanding of whom Jesus is.

> *He is the image of the invisible God,*
> *The first born over all creation.*
> *For in him everything was created,*
> *Everything in heaven and on the earth,*
> *The visible and the invisible,*
> *Whether thrones or powers,*
> *Whether rulers or authorities,*
> *Everything was created through him and for him.*
>
> *He is before all things,*
> *And in him, everything is united.*
>
> *He is the head of his body, the gathering,*
> *Who is the beginning,*
> *The first born from the dead.*

---

[2] James R. Harrison. (2002). Paul and the Imperial Gospel in Thessaloniki. *Journal for the Study of the New Testament* 25(1):71-96, p.78.

So that he might be supreme in everything.

For God was pleased to have his fullness dwell in him,
And through him reconcile everything to himself,
To make peace through the blood of his cross,
Whether with things on the earth
Or things in heaven.

Colossians 1:15-20

This poem is full of echoes of the Hebrew Scriptures, full of allusions to the story of the people of God and his dealing with them. But at the same time it is a clear challenge to the power of the Roman Empire.[3] Paul was writing in a society that was full of images of the Emperor, who was taken to be son of god. Paul subverts the word 'gathering,' which in the society of the day normally meant a political institution (and in most modern translations is translated 'church'). Rome was viewed at the head of those gatherings, Rome was the souce of peace, the city whose imperial might united all lands and peoples in peace. But Paul says, no, it is Christ who does this; he is the creator, the redeemer, the source of peace. The power of the empire is limited, it is finite, it is less than that of a crucified Jew whom hardly anyone had ever heard of.

Yet despite his argument in Philippians and Colossians that Jesus, not the emperor, is Lord, Paul writes in Romans 13 that the authorities are to be respected. Having exhorted Christians to imitate Christ in Romans 12, to renew their minds, to serve and love one another, Paul also exhorts civil obedience. His argument runs as follows:

Everyone must submit to the governing authorities,
for there is no authority except that from God. The
authorities that exist are established by God. Therefore,

---

[3] This discussion of Colossians is shaped by Brian J. Walsh and Sylvia C. Keesmaat, *Colossians re:mixed*, pp.83-84.

> whoever resists the authorities is resisting what God has established, and those who do so will bring judgement on themselves. For rulers hold no fear for those who do right, but those who do wrong. If you want to not fear those in authority, then do good, and he will praise you. For he is God's servant for your good. But if you do wrong, then fear, for he does not have a sword for nothing. He is God's servant, an agent of wrath for those who do wrong. Therefore it is necessary to submit to the authorities, not only because of wrath but also because of conscience.

Romans 13:1-5

But this is not a contradiction. At the heart of Paul's understanding of and engagement with the Roman Empire, then, is this idea that all authority is ultimately God given. The authorities are God's servants, tasked with maintaining God's rule and bringing divine justice to bear on God's world. The Roman authorities may have failed to understand who Jesus is, but that is not a license for civil disobedience. But neither is it a reason to submit completely to their power, as they should be acting in a way that makes it clear they are God's servants. Elsewhere Paul tells slaves to take their freedom if they can obtain it (1 Corinthians 7:21); he expects masters to love and care for their slaves (Colossians 4:1) and even to free them (Philemon). Paul is clear that worship should be given to God alone. Authoritiy is God given, and must be used in accordance with the divine mandate; exceeding one's own authority is as much a sin as failing to exercise it at all.

Worship in the Roman Empire

Having discussed how Paul subverts the claims of the Roman Empire in his letters, I will now turn to a specific real-life problem for many of the first gentile converts to Christianity. The issue of worship and relationship with the temples of the different pagan cults was one that particularly concerned many new Christians in the first century, and so Paul responds to this concern a number of times in his writing. One place where it was a topic of discussion was Corinth.

A typical visitor to the ancient city of Corinth would have approached the city along the paved stones of the Lechaion Road. On the right stood the great Temple of Apollo, built in the 6th century BCE; seven of its Doric columns still stand silhouetted against the Aegean sun. Only a few steps from the temple were the sacred springs of the Pierenne, where pilgrims had worshipped for centuries. Towering over the entire metropolis was the Acrocorinth, an immense outcropping that sheltered shrines sacred to the goddesses Aphrodite and Demeter. There were temples everywhere.

Sitting astride an isthmus, Corinth served two harbours: Lechaion to the north and Cenchreae to the East. Along the shipping lanes and through the bustling warehouses passed luxury goods such as leather, linen, wine, oils and fine marble that appealed to the tastes of the city's wealthy residents. Religious practice followed trade routes. Besides Apollo, Athena, Aphrodite, and Asclepius, the residents of Corinth paid homage to foreign as well as civic deities.[4]

Ben Witherington describes Corinth as follows:

> Corinth was a city where public boasting and self-promotion had become an art form. The Corinthian people lived within an honour-shame cultural orientation, where public recognition was often more important than facts and were the worst thing that could happen was for one's

---

[4] Taken from http://www.pbs.org/wgbh/pages/frontline/shows/religion/maps/arch/corinth.html.

reputation to be publicly tarnished. In such a culture a person's sense of worth is based on recognition by others of one's accomplishments.[5]

Paul worked with his hands, but well-to-do aristocratic Romans, like Greeks, often had a low opinion of those who practiced a trade, and many of Paul's problems in Corinth seem to have been caused by the wealthy and the social climbers among the Corinthians who were upset at him for not meeting their expectations for a great orator and teacher. Corinth was a city where an enterprising person could rise quickly in society through the accumulation and judicious use of newfound wealth. Witherington suggests that it seems that in Paul's time many in Corinth were suffering from a self-made-person-escapes-humble-origins syndrome and so 'in a city where social climbing was a major preoccupation, Paul's deliberate stepping down in apparent status would have been seen by many as disturbing, disgusting, and even provocative.'[6]

One of the many issues that new Christians confronted in Corinth was what to do when the imperial cult celebrated with games and athletics and parties in temples. Should they participate, and so worship the emperor, or should they abstain, and so become socially ostracised?

Paul responds:

> *Concerning food sacrificed to idols, we know that we have all knowledge. Knowledge puffs up but love builds up. The person who thinks he knows something does not yet know what he ought to know. But whoever loves God is known by him. So concerning the eating of food sacrificed to idols, we know that an idol is not anything*

[5] Ben Witherington III. (1995). *Conflict and Community in Corinth: A Socio-Rhetorical Commentary on 1 and 2 Corinthians.* Grand Rapids: Eerdmans, p.8.
[6] Ben Witherington, *Conflict and Community*, p.21.

> *in this world, and we know that there is no god but the One. For even if there are so-called 'gods,' whether in heaven or on earth (as indeed there are many 'gods' and many 'lords'), yet there is for us but One God, the Father, from whom everything came, and for whom we live. And there is one Lord Jesus Christ, from whom everything came, and for whom we live.*
>
> *But not everyone knows this. Some people are still so used to idols, that when they eat food sacrificed to idols, since their consciences are weak, they think of it as being defiled. But food does not bring us closer to God. We are no worse if we do not eat and no better if we do.*
>
> *Watch out that your authority in this does not become a stumbling block to the weak. For if someone with a weak conscience sees you eating in an idol's temple, won't he feel bold enough to eat food sacrificed to idols? So this weak one is destroyed by your knowledge, a fellow-believer for whom Christ died. When you sin against your fellow-believers in this way, and wound their weak consciences, you sin against Christ. Therefore if what I eat causes a fellow-believer to stumble into sin, I will never eat meat again, so I do not cause him to fall.*
>
> 1 Corinthians 8:1-13

Paul's argument concerns the proper use of knowledge. It is all very well to know that idols do not actually exist. It is commendable to have come to the realisation that the One God is the only true God, and that idols are false. But the question remains, will this intellectual knowledge become a source of pride that is in fact detrimental to individual and corporate Christian faith?

Paul acknowledges the diversity of religious opinion in his day: there are many so-called 'gods' and 'lords,' to whom different people claim allegiance. But Christians serve only the Father and his Son, Jesus Christ. Notice how Paul uses exactly the same language to refer to the Father and the Son, making it clear that he regards them as One God.

Although Paul is clear that Jesus is Lord, the One God, not everyone, not even every Christian, has fully understood what this means. For some, perhaps those who have only recently become Christians, the idea of idols being real, the idea that they actually represent a god who can change the course of history, means that whenever they eat food that has been offered to an idol, their conscience condemns them. Paul is clear this is not actually a valid condemnation. Food is something you eat and that is all. What you eat does not bring you closer to God, nor does it distance you from him. But Paul is not concerned simply with intellectual knowledge, but with the application of that knowledge to daily living. Will individual knowledge build up the fellowship of believers, or will it tear them down?

Paul uses the idea of authority to make his point clear: will those with authority as more knowledgeable, more experienced Christians, care for those whose faith is still in its infancy? Or will they exercise their freedom for their own gain, regardless of how it impacts others? His point is that my personal knowledge that a course of action is justifiable does not mean I should necessarily act in that way, especially not if my public display of freedom will cause other Christians, who regard those actions as sinful, to do the same themselves. Freedom is not individual, it is corporate, Paul argues. We are responsible not just for our own relationship with Jesus, but for the relationship all the Christians we know have with him.

What Paul wants the Corinthian Christians to realise is that their personal gain within the Roman Empire is of much less importance that the security of Christian believers within Jesus' alternative empire. We each have one master, and we must serve him and care for our fellow-believers, even if this costs us personally.

Questions

1. What relationship should Christians have with those in authority in the UK today? In what way are the British Government agents of divine justice? How are they going against divine teaching?

2. What rights do we have as British citizens that we can use to promote the Gospel of Jesus Christ? Do we take advantage of those rights?

3. What challenges are there to being a Christian that are unique to living in the UK?

4. Thinking about Paul's example of food offered to idols, what freedom do we have as a Christian that we should choose to not exercise out of loyalty to Jesus' Alterative Empire?

I can, but I won't

'So why aren't you going to the pub?'

Will was looking a bit confused, and maybe even a tiny bit angry. His forehead was creased, his eyes slightly narrowed, and his head turned a bit to one side, in a quizzical, "what is all this about?" sort of a way.

'I mean, you're quite happy to have a pint or two, aren't you?'

'Yeah,' I nodded. 'As you know, I hate lager, but if it is worth drinking, then, yes, I am quite happy to drink a pint or two of it.'

'And you're not facing a deadline tonight? I mean, no more than normal?'

'No,' I shook my head, confirming that I was no further behind with my work than I normally was on a Wednesday afternoon. Two more days to catch up and keep my head above water. It ought to be fine. It had been every other week for the past twenty years, seven months and one week. Not that I'm counting how long before I can retire or anything, you understand.

'There's no urgent thing calling you home is there?'

'Well, only my wife and daughters.'

'Obviously,' Will gestured to accept that possible excuse. 'But that doesn't stop you having one drink does it? I can understand you want to be home soon, but it's a ten minute walk, so out the door by five past, pint in the hand by ten past, you can still be home by six.' This plan was accompanied by a few gestures, a sweep of the hand for leaving, a cupped hand to the mouth for the drink (which he seemed to down in about five seconds) and two walking fingers wending their way home to the loving embrace of my family.

'Yeah, that's all true, but I'm still not going today. Said I'd walk home with George. A promise is a promise.'

'Can't he come?'

'He could. But he shouldn't. And I'm not going to invite him, and neither should you, if you care about him at all.'

'What?'

'I ain't saying any more.' I closed the discussion with a sweep of my hands and swung back round in my chair to face my computer screen.

How do you explain that George is the kind of guy for whom a drink comes in fifteen glasses and a trip to A&E? I've known that about him for more than five years, five sober years, and I made a promise to help that happen by being the bad guy if needs be. Will does not have the emotional intelligence to pick up on these subtleties. To him, I'm just a killjoy. Which may not be entirely untrue. I was looking forward to being home before 5:30, and hearing all about the intricacies of the playground debates that my daughters share every evening meal.

The thing is, the fact that you *can* do something is not permission to do it. Of course I can go to the pub any time I want. Of course I can have a drink if I want. But George cannot and since I am his friend, that means I cannot either. But explaining that is not always easy, especially as I want to respect his right to dignity and privacy.

'Ok, whatever, your loss.' Will wandered off, dismissing me with a wave.

Actually, I thought to myself, George's gain.

This story tries to give a modern-day example of caring for a Christian sibling, of choosing not to do something that is not wrong in and of itself solely because you want to avoid causing harm to a fellow believer. The question of who is weak and strong may complicate things, as sometimes a greater sensitivity and relationship with the Spirit can lead Christians to make choices that others might regard simply as the choice of a weak conscience. The balance of being in, but not of, the world is a difficult one that most Christians struggle to maintain.

Chapter 7

Revelation And Empire

It is difficult to be sure exactly what level of persecution that Christians faced towards the end of the first century. Although some scholars argue that there was not a systematic program of state-sponsored, empire-wide persecution, even they accept that it was likely that there were local pockets of extreme persecution, with Christians facing the threat of death if they did not turn away from their faith in Jesus. This means that in some places there was a clear conflict between the Roman Empire and the alternative empire that John, the author of Revelation, believed Jesus founded.

Not Of This World

Craig Koester identifies a number of issues faced by the churches addressed in the book of Revelation. The two main ones were open hostility and the temptation to assimilation.

He further adds the other challenge of worship of the emperor.[1] I will summarise his points on each in turn.

First, some people were openly hostile to Christianity, regarding it as 'a new and mischievous superstition' that needed to be suppressed for the sake of good order in society.[2] Accordingly, Christians could be put in prison for questioning, and if they proved to be noncompliant, they could be put to death at the direction of the Roman proconsul. This is seen elsewhere in the New Testament, such as in Acts 16:19-24; 17:5-9; and implied in Hebrews 10:32-34.

Second, Koester explains that Christians lived in cities where most people still held to traditional religious beliefs. Some of the most popular events in public life were the festivals honoring local deities such as Artemis, Athena, or Dionysus. At the heart of a typical festival was a procession in which animals adorned with ribbons or garlands were led through the crowds of onlookers to the place of sacrifice. After the animals were properly slaughtered according to traditional rites, there were often banquets hosted by civic officials and wealthy benefactors where the meat was served. Such situations presented complex social issues for Christians: How fully can you participate in forms of public life that conflict with your own faith convictions?

And the problem was not limited to public events, as private social gatherings could also have religious aspects, which just made things more difficult. Greco-Roman temples sometimes had dining facilities where people could share meals that included meat from sacrifices offered to a god or goddess. Family celebrations commemorating a birthday or a child's coming of age might be held in a temple's dining

---

[1] Craig Koester. (2009). Revelation's Visionary Challenge to Ordinary Empire. *Interpretation* 63(1): 5-18, pp.6-11. What follows in this section is based on his argument.

[2] Koester, Revelation's Visionary Challenge, p.7 attributes this to Suetonius, Nero 16.2 and suggests other references as Tacitus, Annals 15.44; Pliny the Younger, Epistles 10.96.8-9.

area. Similarly, trade guilds and business associations had gatherings that included rites honoring a particular goddess or god. What were Christians to do if their friends or business associates expected them to take part in gatherings involving beliefs they did not accept? Was it best to maintain your social and business connections, even when this meant suppressing your faith? Or was it better to be clear about your faith and refrain from participating, even if this brought the risk of heightened tensions with non-Christians or ostracism from them?

The third main issue was worship of the emperor. Koester notes that the cult of the emperor was established in Asia Minor at the request of the province. They built a temple to Augustus in 29 BC in Pergamum. Later a second temple was built to Tiberius, in Smyrna, in 23 AD. Moreover, during the 80s AD, the city of Ephesus gained prestige within the Empire by building a provincial temple to Domitian and other members of the imperial family. Worship of the emperor centred upon emphasising military prowess. It did not replace traditional forms of worship but functioned along with them. At Ephesus, for example, joint religious rites honored the goddess Demeter and the emperors. At Pergamum, a festival to the emperor was held in the sacred precincts of the saviour god Asclepius. These are the cities where the Christians addressed in the opening chapters of Revelation lived, and so these were the issues that Revelation challenges, encouraging Christians to refrain from worshipping the emperor, and to remain distinctively and identifiably Christian in the face of rising hostility.

David Barr argues that Revelation is quite blunt in its critique of the Roman Empire. He suggests Revelation does this in two ways: through the use of satirical images and through irony. I will begin by looking at the three inter-related images which Barr argues clearly disparage the might of Rome.[3]

---

[3] David Barr. (2009). John's Ironic Empire. *Interpretation* 63(1): 20-30, pp.24-26.

The first image is that of Babylon, which is found four times (Revelation 14:8; 16:19; 17:5; 18:2, 10, 21). John is using Old Testament imagery to remind his readers of Rome's involvement in the destruction of Jerusalem and the temple, and to invoke divine justice (compare the oracles against Babylon in Isaiah 47; Jeremiah 51-52 and Ezekiel 25-27 with that against Babylon in Revelation 18).

The second, related, image is of a prostitute (Revelation 17:1, 5, 15; 19:2). Not a trafficked woman, not a slave held against her will in a brothel, but a woman of high social standing, permitted to wear purple and gold, a woman of whom much should be expected. John is probably parodying the goddess Roma, mocking her for getting drunk on the blood of martyrs and pointing out the corruption at the heart of the Roman system.

The third image is that of the beast. The beast is said to rule over the whole world (Revelation 13:1-8), an allusion to the all-encompassing power of Rome. This beast is supported by a second beast, whom Barr suggests represents the elite rulers of Asia Minor. The second beast supports the first, and establishes worship of him (Revelation 13:11-15). The image of the beast occurs elsewhere in the book of Revelation, always as an evil presence reminiscent of the might of Rome.

Satirical imagery is not enough. John also critiques Rome by using irony. A lot of the central scenes in Revelation are scenes of worship of a triumphant, exalted king, but in stark contrast to imperial Rome, the kingdom is founded not on dominant military power, but weakness and sacrifice. John's use of irony is the means by which he sets out his understanding of Jesus' alternative empire.[4] Thus for example in the letters to the churches in chapters two and three, there is the irony that those who appear rich are really poor and those who appear poor are really rich (3:17; 2:9). Moreover

[4] This suggestion is based on the reading of John's irony found in Barr, *John's Ironic Empire*, pp.29-30.

each of the seven communities must conquer but in this story, conquest comes only through death (2:10). The grand heavenly figure does not intervene on their behalf and does not rescue them. He only talks and promises them victory on the most unlikely of terms: continuing to do his work (2:26), work that entailed his death.

Second, in the heavenly vision of chapters four and five, Rome's rule is overturned by John's vision of the true throne in heaven, shared by God and the lamb. When we look behind his throne, we see it is the death of Jesus that gives this throne power: 'You are worthy to take the scroll and to open its seals, for you were slaughtered and by your blood you ransomed for God saints from every tribe and language and people and nation' (5:9). Those who read the empire of Jesus as an imitation of the empire of Rome fail to take due note of how he attained the throne: the 'worthy lamb' is declared ruler when his only accomplishment has been to die.

Third, the seemingly powerless and oppressed followers of Jesus in Asia Minor really are a vast army of 144,000 virgin warriors (14:1-5). But if we look behind this image, we see them as 'firstfruits' and 'blameless', both traits of a proper sacrifice (Leviticus 2:14-3:2), slaughtered for others. The audience knows what the dragon and his armies cannot know, that the battle is already over and they have lost. But the audience also knows what the heavenly warriors do not: only their blood will purchase their victory (12:11).

At the heart of Revelation is an ironic re-reading of power, a challenge to the power of the Roman Empire through a demonstration of the power of the alternative empire. But that power is based on weakness and death: it is only when you look behind the scenes of history that you realise exactly what is going on. Jesus is powerful, and his empire will prevail. But the basis of his power and the way in which the empire prevails is nothing like that of the world. Weakness and sacrifice are everything; claims to dominance and authority count for nothing. The alternative empire is founded on the power of weakness and the glorious suffering of Christ and his followers.

Seeing What Is Really There

Revelation draws back the curtain of history to show us the reality of creation. The main aim of the book is to remind us that even though we face trouble, even though it seems that the empires of this age are all powerful, the reality is that they are defeated, that Jesus has triumphed, and we are on the winning side. As Richard Bewes' commentary puts it, 'The Lamb Wins.'[5]

In this detailed look at certain extracts from the book of Revelation, I have included a number of short extracts that illustrate David Barr's argument about how Revelation supports the alternative empire.[6]

First, the Letter to the church in Smyrna:

> And to the angel of the church in Smyrna write: the one who is the first and the last, who was dead and is alive says these things: I know your suffering and your poverty, though you are rich and the blasphemy of those saying they are Jews and are not but are a synagogue of Satan. Do not fear that which you are about to suffer. Behold the devil is about to throw some of you into prison so that you will suffer for ten days. Remain faithful until death and I will give you the crown of life. Let him who has an ear hear what the

---

[5] Richard Bewes. (2000). *The Lamb Wins*. Fearne: Christian Focus.

[6] The comments on the four passages are a combination of my own thoughts with reading G. K. Beale. (1999). *New International Greek Testament Commentary: The Book of Revelation*. Grand Rapids: Eerdmans.

Spirit is saying to the churches. The victor will surely
not be harmed by the second death.

Revelation 2:8-11

John writes to explain to them that in spite of their apparent poverty they are actually rich. If they endure faithfully, they will be rewarded, although they will experience further persecution. The central issue addressed is likely to have been Christian refusal to pay homage to the emperor as a deity. Those refusing to do so would be regarded as politically disloyal and unpatriotic. The behaviour of the Jews in Smyrna (who presumably are complying and worshipping) shows they are false, a 'synagogue of Satan,' and that in contrast the church was the 'true Israel.'

The reference to 'ten days of tribulation' may be an allusion to Daniel 1:12-15, where Daniel and his friends are tested for ten days to determine if they could remain healthy without eating the king's rich food. The Christians in Smyrna are encouraged that they will be victorious, but only in and through death, not through any attempt to exert their own abilities.

Second, the church in Philadelphia:

And to the angel of the church in Philadelphia write: the
Holy One, the True, who has the key of David, who opens
and no one will shut, and shuts and no one opens, says
this: I know your deeds, I have given you an open door,
which no one will be able to shut, because you have
a little power and keep my word and do not deny my
name. Behold I will give those of the synagogue of Satan,
who call themselves Jews and are not. Behold I will make
them come and bow before your feet and they will know
that I have loved you. Therefore keep to the word of my
obedience and I will keep you in the hour of testing that
is coming to test all those who dwell in the whole earth.

*I am coming soon. Hold fast to what you have, so that no
one can take your crown. I will make the victor a pillar
in the temple of my God and you will never go out of
it and I will write on him the name of my God and the
name of the city of my God, the new Jerusalem, which
is come down from heaven from my God, and my new
name. Let he who has an ear listen to what the Spirit is
saying to the churches.*

Revelation 3:7-13

John explains to the Christians in Philadelphia that although they are numerically insignificant, they are being
used by Christ and if they remain faithful to him he will reward them in due time. Christ, the true witness and sovereign
over the realms of life and death, exercises his power in the
area on behalf of the Philadelphian church, granting its members the right to enter eternal life. The promise in 3:9 is God's
promise—'I will make them in order that they will come and
bow down before your feet' is a collective allusion to Isaiah
45:14; 49:23; 60:14; Psalm 86:9. All these Old Testament texts
predict the Gentiles will come and bow down before Israel
and Israel's God in the last days. This prophecy has been fulfilled ironically in the Gentile church, which has become true
Israel by virtue of its faith in Christ. The reference to believers receiving a crown may develop further the use of Isaiah
22, where God promises to take away evil Shebna's crown
and give it to faithful Eliakim (Isaiah 22:15-24). The warning
to hold fast expresses an expectation that tough times will
come, making it clear that being a citizen of the alternative
empire is not easy.

Third, John's vision of worship in heaven:

*And I saw in the right hand of the one seated on the
throne a scroll written on inside and out, sealed up with
seven seals. And I saw a mighty angel crying out in a*

loud voice, "Who is worthy to open the scroll and to remove its seals?" And no one in heaven nor on the earth nor under the earth was able to open the scroll or look inside it. And I wept greatly because no one worthy was found to open the scroll or look inside it. And one of the elders said to me, "Do not weep, behold, the lion of the tribe of Judah has triumphed, the root of David, to open the scroll and its seven seals."

And I saw in the midst of the throne and of the four living creatures and in the midst of the elders, a lamb standing, as though slain, with seven horns and seven eyes, which is the seven-fold Spirit of God sent into all the earth. And he came and received it from the right hand of the one seated on the throne. And when he took the scroll, the four living creatures and the twenty four elders fell down before the lamb, each with a harp and a golden bowl filled with incense, which is the prayers of the saints, and they sang a new song saying, "You are worthy to receive the scroll and open its seals, because you were slain and purchased for God with your blood people from every tribe and language and people and nation and you have made them a kingdom and priests for our God, and they will reign on the earth."

And I looked and heard the voices of many angels around the throne and the living creatures and the elders; they numbered myriads upon myriads and thousands upon thousands, saying in loud voices, "Worthy is the lamb who was slain to receive power and riches and wisdom and strength, and honour and glory and praise."

And I heard all the creatures that are in heaven and on the earth and under the earth and in the sea and everything that is in them saying, "To the one seated on the throne and to the lamb, blessing and honour, glory and power, for ever and ever."

> *And the four living creatures said "Amen." And the*
> *elders fell down and worshipped.*
>
> Revelation 5:1-14

The irony here is striking. John looks for a lion, a dominant, royal, powerful predator, and as he turns he sees an already slaughtered lamb, a submissive, poor, weak herbivore. The message is clear: there is strength in willing self-sacrifice that no imperial Roman might can defeat. Worship should be directed in the proper direction: towards the worthy lamb who gave everything up for us.

Fourth, the vision of the martyrs who are the first fruits:

> *And I looked and behold, the Lamb was standing on*
> *Mount Zion, and with him the 144 000 who have his*
> *name and his father's name written on their foreheads.*
> *And I heard a voice from heaven like the sound of many*
> *waters and of a great thunder and the voices which I*
> *heard were like harpists playing their harps. And they*
> *sang a new song before the throne and before the four*
> *living creatures and the elders, and no one was able to*
> *learn the song except for the 144 000, those purchased*
> *from the earth. They are those who have not defiled*
> *themselves with women, for they are virgins, those who*
> *follow the Lamb wherever he goes. Those who were*
> *purchased from humanity, the first fruits to God and to*
> *the Lamb, and no lie is found in their mouths, for they*
> *are blameless.*
>
> Revelation 14:1-5

Here the Lamb is compared with the two beasts, making the contrast between the true and false objects of worship clear. God has installed him on Mount Zion with all his chosen people: the number 144 000 connotes the completeness of God's chosen people, marked as his own, in antithesis to the 666 on the foreheads of the beast's followers (13:18). The saints all praise God, singing a new song, a sign of his victory (Psalm 40:3; 98:1; Isaiah 42:10). The characteristics of these saints are then also spelt out further: they are those who have kept themselves pure and unpolluted by the world, taking on the characteristics of the messianic servant (Isaiah 53:7, 9; Zephaniah 3:11-14).

Questions

As you read through these four passages ask yourself:

1. What do these passages teach us about whom Jesus is?

2. How powerful do you think the Christians described in these passages are? Do you find anything in them that echoes your own experience?

3. What do the letters and visions of heaven teach us about the reality of our current situation?

4. How can we learn to see things not as the world does, but as God does?

Blind But Not Helpless

'Sorry, if you want to shake my hand, you'll have to be a bit more decisive and grasp it firmly.'

I froze, hand only partially extended. What did he mean?

Light dawned with his explanation, although light was something he never saw. 'I'm blind,' the reverend smiled, turning his head slightly so his sightless white eyeballs were more directly in my view. 'I'm not psychic, nor am I super sensitive to movement,' he went on, answering the question that was only part way formed in my mind. 'It's just experience. Whenever people meet me for the first time, they always extend a hand expecting me to take it. For a long time I didn't realise, and so people's hands were just extended and empty. Then a kind lady in the congregation told me it was happening, so now I always make that offer. Do please take my hand, I'd love to shake yours.'

I took the partly extended hand hesitantly, and he grasped mine firmly. 'Lovely to meet you. I'm sorry for startling you. I hope it hasn't made you feel uncomfortable. Shall we go and sit down?'

Normally a handshake in greeting lasts less that ten seconds. This was much longer and he still held mine. But it wasn't uncomfortable. In fact it was reassuring. I looked around for some chairs and spotted two, close to other, with a small table between them. 'I think I can see some where suitable, shall I lead the way?' I offered.

'Yes please, just swap hands so it is easier to walk.'

I did as instructed and we were soon comfortably settled in two church chairs, each with arms. The reverend rested his hands lightly on the arms of his chair, almost as if it were a resassuring friend. 'It is always good to hold someone's hand when you're blind,' he smiled.

'Tea or coffee?'

I started and gasped again. The voice came from over my left shoulder. I had not heard anyone. But there was a lady who looked to be in her early thirties, careful make up, a wisp of blond hair escaping from a pony tail and caressing her left cheek.

'Um, tea please. Milk but no sugar.'

'Usual for you Father?'

'Yes, thank you Caroline. Sorry, I think we've startled our friend again. I apologise that my lack of eyes is doing your heart no good,' he said with a hint of a smile. 'And I'm sorry that I don't think I know your name? I'm Father Christopher,' he added, turning his hands up and opening them in a gesture of welcome.

'I'm Susan, Susan Okellor, from Uganda. Please forgive me, but I have never met a blind reverend before, and it has startled me.' I blushed at my own bluntness. But that has always been my way, to say exactly what I am thinking, even when doing so has resulted in embarrassment or trouble. Forgetting what I had come for for a moment, I continued my interrogation.

'How can you celebrate Holy Communion if you are blind? How do you baptise the infants? What about a burial? Wouldn't you fall into the grave?' A river of questions fountained out, stemmed only by Caroline arriving back with our drinks. Her blond hair, it made me jealous of my own black short curls. She put my drink on the table and with a practised 'Here you are Father,' handed him a mug which he grasped easily in his outstretch hand. The palm of his other hand was raised to forestall any further questions.

'So many questions Susan, so many. Let me see if I can answer them all this way.' He paused, taking a sip from his steaming cup. He smacked his lips. 'Ah, that's good. Caroline always makes my tea just the way I like it. I think that's my answer.'

'Sorry?' My forehead was knotted with confusion. 'Caroline makes your tea?'

'Yes,' the reverend smiled. 'The chief server, Chris, guides my hands to the plate and the chalice. The mother always places the baby in my hands carefully and again

Chris guides my hand with the water. The funeral directors all know me. They all guide me, explaining to the family what they are doing and why. My useless eyes are a real blessing to the church, even if they are a source of pain to me.'

The fog of misunderstanding was both clearer and denser, all at once. 'You mean, people help you?' I ventured.

'Oh yes, all that and much more. People give more of themselves in the service of Christ because they know I cannot. I cannot welcome new people, so they do so, and guide them to me. I guess that happened to you on your way here?'

'Yes.' I realised that as I had hesitantly entered the church three people had all smiled their hellos, had all asked whom I wanted to see and had all pointed me to the reverend.

'And,' he continued, 'when I talk with my colleagues, it seems we have far more volunteers in our congregation than are often present in a community of our size. People know what I cannot do, and so they do it for me. We always have people who want to serve at mass, always have a verger, always have someone to take me to meeting when I ask, at least when I ask for the fifth time.' He grinned.

'Yes, I would love to be able to see. The world going dark as my eyes failed in my mid twenties was the most painful part of my life, but I've shouted enough at the Father about it for the last thirty years, and I know his power is made perfect in my weakness, and most of the time I can even accept it. I may look weak, but the Father is using me for his Kingdom. But enough about me, what did you want us to help you with Susan?'

I explained about my son, about baptism, how things had turned out and why now, before his fourth birthday, I wanted it to happen. I had been dreading going, dreading having to explain my failure for the past three and a half years. But the reverend father was so kind, so gentle as he explained that his was a Catholic church, not the Anglican one I had mistaken it for. That made no difference to me. Their family seemed so warm, I wanted the baptism to be there.

'Of course we can,' his smile reassured me. 'You'll have to attend classes together and Stephen must be a good boy and stand very still for me when the time comes to pour the water. But we would love to welcome you into our family.'

And they did. A fractious family, full of arguments at times, but always conscious of where we were weak and where we could help each other. A wonderful family to have joined.

This story explores the theme of strength in weakness. I would not want to make patronising statements of how a weakness in one area is compensated for by strength in others (so the priest's blindness means his congregation are perhaps slightly more willing to volunteer than normal, but not excessively so). The point is more that things are not how they seem at first, that what was initially thought of as weakness might actually be an opportunity to encourage collaboration and sharing within ministry.

One of the key points of Revelation is that the Church is not the weak organisation she may appear to be when viewed only through human eyes. We need to learn to see things with a more eternal perspective.

www.ingramcontent.com/pod-product-compliance
Lightning Source LLC
Chambersburg PA
CBHW070814050426
42452CB00011B/2040